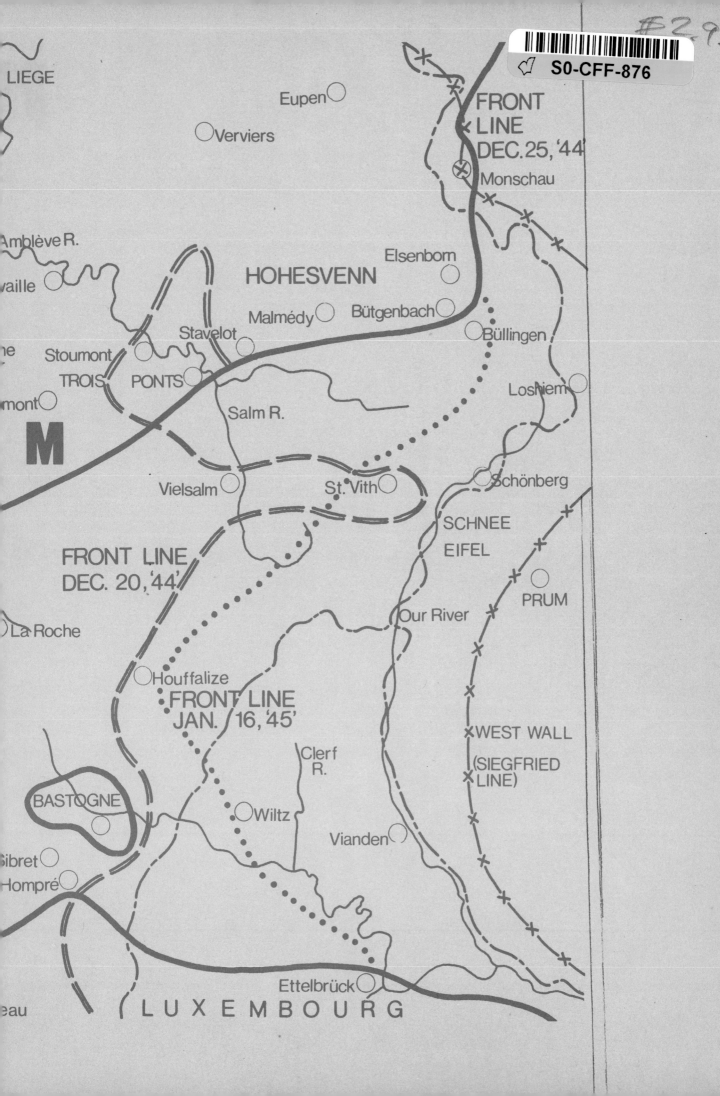

$2.95

LIEGE

Eupen○

○Verviers

Amblève R.

Elsenborn○

vaille○

HOHESVENN

Malmédy○ Bütgenbach○

Stavelot○ Büllingen○

Stoumont○

TROIS PONTS

Loshiem○

Salm R.

M

Vielsalm○ St. Vith○ Schönberg○

SCHNEE
EIFEL

FRONT LINE
DEC. 20, '44'

Our River PRUM○

○La Roche

WEST WALL

○Houffalize FRONT LINE
JAN. 16, '45'

(SIEGFRIED
LINE)

Clerf
R.

BASTOGNE

○Wiltz

Vianden○

Sibret○

Hompré○

FRONT
LINE
DEC. 25, '44'

⊗ Monschau

Ettelbrück○

L U X E M B O U R G

eau

BATTLE OF THE BULGE
1944

BATTLE OF THE BULGE 1944

Napier Crookenden

Charles Scribner's Sons
NEW YORK

Acknowledgements

The search for photographs, paintings and drawings with which to illustrate this short account of the Battle of the Ardennes has been a real pleasure, because of the friendly, effective and sympathetic help which I have received in each of the three main sources, American, German and British. The United States Air Force Photographic Squadron provided me with several excellent photographs and in the United States Army Audio Visual Activity at the Pentagon, the kindness and help of Mrs Viola Destefano and her ladies made light of my task of looking through several thousand Army photographs. Across the river at 2nd and S Streets Mrs Marian McNaughton gave me invaluable aid in sifting through the US War Department's collection of war artists' works – and as before, I had the benefit of a lot of help and sound advice from the Chief of Military History, Brig-Gen James L. Collins.

In Koblenz Doctor Haupt and his staff at the Bundesarchiv could not have been more helpful, and at the Imperial War Museum in London Robert Crawford and all the staff of the Department of Photographs made every visit a pleasure—as they always do.

I have based this summary of the battle on the detailed, and balanced, Ardennes volume of the *United States Army in World War II*, written so clearly and readably by Dr Hugh M. Cole, but I am also very much indebted to John S. D. Eisenhower's gripping and vivid account of the battle in his book *The Bitter Woods*. Much of the detail in the Bastogne chapter comes from Brig-Gen Marshall's compelling book *The First Eight Days* and I have been helped too by Lt-Gens William R. Desobry and Julian J. Ewell.

I am grateful also to Messieurs Schmitz-Damman and Joss Heintz of Bastogne for sending me a copy of M Heintz's book *In the Perimeter of Bastogne* and to Mr Tom Fitch of the Parachute Regiment and Airborne Forces Museum at Aldershot.

If anyone wants to follow in more detail the dramatic fortunes of Jochen Peiper's battlegroup of the 1st SS Panzer Division, they can do no better than read Charles Whiting's *Malmedy Massacre*.

The maps were drawn by Andrew Snell and without Mrs Moore's accurate typing, the book would never have been finished.

Contents

1 The German Plan for a Counter Offensive

On 16 September 1944, the day before Field Marshal Montgomery's airborne and armoured drive into Holland began, Adolf Hitler called a conference at his East Prussian headquarters, the 'Wolf's Lair'. His two chief service advisers were there as usual, Field Marshal Wilhelm Keitel and Gen Alfred Jodl, together with Gen Heinz Guderian, the acting Chief of Staff of the Army and Gen Werner Kreipe, the Air Force Chief of Staff. Kreipe was representing Hermann Goering and kept full notes of the proceedings.

After the usual daily briefing on current events at the main battle fronts, Jodl outlined the general situation and included the estimate that 96 Allied divisions were now facing 55 German divisions on the Western Front. Ten more Allied divisions were known to be on their way to the front from the United Kingdom, where there were also five Allied airborne divisions. Three of these, unknown to the Germans, were to drop next day at Eindhoven, Nijmegen and Arnhem. As soon as Jodl had finished his brief, Hitler announced: 'I have just made a momentous decision. I shall go over to the counter-attack here – out of the Ardennes – with objective Antwerp.'

His audience were shocked into silence. They were well aware of Germany's desperate position and Guderian was particularly concerned with the need to concentrate Germany's remaining strength against the advancing Russians. The Russian threat to East Prussia and to Germany's eastern provinces, the homeland of so many German regular officers, was regarded much more seriously by the army than was the Allied pressure from the West.

Germany was alone. Italy had been defeated and was now on the side of the Allies; Japan was suggesting peace overtures to the Russians; Romania and Bulgaria had switched to the side of the Russians and Finland had broken off her uneasy alliance with Germany. 1,200,000 German soldiers, sailors and airmen were dead, wounded or missing and another 230,000 were surrounded in the French ports. The Russians were almost up to the borders of East Prussia; the German Army was retreating in Greece and Yugoslavia; in Italy the British and American armies had reached the Po valley; the Allies were well into Holland; and the United States Ninth and First Armies were already in Germany, approaching Aachen. Every day 5,000 Allied aircraft were over Germany and although the bombing offensive had not yet sapped the German will to fight, or reduced the flow of armaments, the air raids had caused terrible casualties and damage in Germany's main cities.

Oil production and ammunition were soon to be affected, but ball bearings, fighter aircraft, tanks and guns were still coming off the production lines at an increasing rate. The German people's morale was stiffened by the Allied leaders' repeated demands for unconditional surrender and the German railway system, on which the new counter-attack was to depend so heavily, was still most effective.

Below left: Oberstgeneral Jodl on his way to Rheims in June 1945 to meet the Allied Chiefs of Staff./*US Army*

Below: Oberstgeneral Keitel at Compiegne after the French surrender in 1940./*Bundesarchiv*

Fired by the example of his hero, Frederic the Great, Hitler was certain that Germany was capable of a decisive blow against the Allies in the west, which would split the Allied armies, disrupt their supply lines and fatally divide their political leadership. He chose the Ardennes for his counter-attack, because the United States divisions there were widely spread, the hills and woods gave cover for the assembly of his forces and it was close to the boundary between the British and American Army Groups. He decided on late November or early December, because bad flying weather would hamper the Allied Air Forces, who now ruled the skies.

In September 1944 the German armed forces numbered over 10,000,000 men in 327 divisions and brigades. Although men were now being called up from 16 to 60, there were still large reserves in the navy and air force and another four million men in reserved occupations. The German armed forces and the army in particular were still a formidable fighting machine.

The German supreme command, the Oberkommando der Wehrmacht (OKW), presented an outline plan on 25 September. On 22 October Field Marshal von Rundstedt's Chief of Staff at Headquarters West, Oberbefehlshaber West, Gen Siegfried Westphal and Gen Hans Krebs, Chief of Staff to the Commander of Army Group B, Field Marshal Model, were summoned in their turn to the 'Wolf's Lair' to be briefed personally by the Führer and to learn that D-Day was to be 25 November. The Sixth and Fifth Panzer Armies and the Seventh Army were to carry out the attack with 12 panzer and one panzer grenadier divisions and 18 infantry divisions, supported by 1,500 fighter and bomber aircraft and supplied with four and a quarter million gallons of fuel and 50 train-loads of ammunition.

To brief chiefs of staff before their commanders was a common German Army practice, but in this case Hitler was proably also influenced by the return of von Rundstedt as Commander-in-Chief West. Although the most respected senior officer in the German Army, his aloof and non-political outlook and his obvious lack of enthusiasm for Nazi ideals led Hitler to regard him as too old and too lukewarm. Main responsibility for launching the attack was given to Field Marshal Walther Model, commanding Army Group B. A brilliant, ambitious and much younger man, Model was an ardent Nazi and a favourite with Hitler. In spite of serious misgivings about Hitler's adventurous plans, he was to lead his Army Group most ably for the remaining months of the war, until its final encirclement and surrender in the Ruhr on 21 April and his own suicide.

The objectives set him by Hitler – Brussels and Antwerp – were in his opinion much too distant for achievement by the available forces and for some days he and his Chief, von Rundstedt, supported by his army commanders, tried to persuade Hitler to accept the more limited aim of driving to the Meuse and then turning north

Above left: Field Marshals Model and von Runstedt and Gen Krebs discuss the Ardennes offensive in November 1944./*Bundesarchiv*

Above: Field Marshal Gerd von Runstedt and Lt-Gen Alexander Patch, US Army, in May 1945 at Augsburg./*US Army*

Left: Field Marshal Walther Model and his aide talking to soldiers in November 1944. /*IWM*

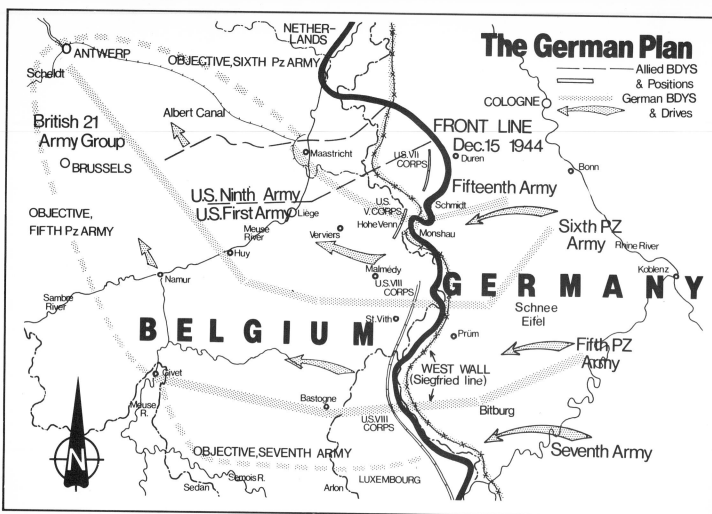

ANTWERP

Scheldt

OBJECTIVE, SIXTH Pz ARMY

NETHER-LANDS

COLOGNE

British 21
Army Group

Albert Canal

Maastricht

U.S.VII
CORPS

Duren

FRONT LINE
Dec.15 1944

Bonn

BRUSSELS

OBJECTIVE,
FIFTH Pz ARMY

U.S. Ninth Army
U.S.First Army

Liège

Meuse
River

Huy

Verviers

U.S.
V.CORPS

Hohe Venn

Schmidt

Monshau

Fifteenth Army

Sixth PZ
Army

Rhine River

Namur

Malmédy
U.S.VIII
CORPS

G E R M A N Y

Koblenz

Sambre
River

B E L G I U M

St.Vith

Prüm

Schnee
Eifel

Givet

Meuse
R.

Bastogne

WEST WALL
(Siegfried line)

Fifth PZ
Army

Bitburg

U.S.VIII
CORPS

Sedan

OBJECTIVE,SEVENTH ARMY

Semois R.

Arlon

LUXEMBOURG

Seventh Army

N

to split the American and British armies. They failed completely
and were sharply ordered by Hitler to press on with the original
plan.

In the north of the Ardennes the Sixth SS Panzer Army was to
cross the Meuse each side of Liège and then wheel north to strike
for the Albert Canal and the line Antwerp-Maastricht. The Army
commander, Sepp Dietrich, had marched with Hitler in the
original Nazi putsch of 1923 and before that had been a sergeant
in World War I. Originally a butcher by trade, he was a big,
burly figure and was regarded by the professionals of the Army as
an over-promoted SS tough. However he had fought in Greece,
Russia and Normandy, was a brave and tenacious leader at divisional and corps level and had wide experience with tanks in battle.
His Sixth SS Panzer Army were now given the priority task on the
right flank in Hitler's grandiose plans and an able, regular soldier,
Fritz Kraemer, took over as his Chief of Staff.

In the centre Gen Hasso-Eccard von Manteuffel's Fifth Panzer
Army were to cross the Meuse at Namur and Dinant and drive for
the line Charleroi-Brussels. Von Manteuffel came from an old
army family. A little over five foot in height he had been a successful amateur rider before the war and had served with tanks since
1936. He had proved his energy, ability and courage in North
Africa and Russia and his staff and troops were devoted to him.
He was one of the few army generals, who was unafraid of Hitler
and was ready to voice disagreement with him or even to tell him
the odd story.

On the left the Seventh Army, led by Gen Brandenberger, was
to make a limited advance to form a defensive line, facing south
and south-west, protecting the left flank of the main thrust by the
two panzer armies.

While the army, corps and divisional commanders were making
their detailed tactical plans under conditions of the strictest secrecy,
the Quartermaster General and the Chief of Transportation of the
German Armed Forces were grappling with the huge task of assem-

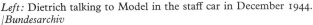

Left: Dietrich talking to Model in the staff car in December 1944. */Bundesarchiv*

Above: Fritz Kraemer as a young lieutenant-colonel./*Bundesarchiv*

Above right: Gen Hasso-Eccard von Manteuffel, talking to a captain. */Bundesarchiv*

Right: Von Manteuffel, Thomale and Model on the Eifel in December 1944./*Bundesarchiv*

bling the men, tanks, weapons, vehicles and stores from all over Germany, from East Prussia and Poland, from Denmark, Norway and Austria. 66 divisions were moved by rail and only seven by road. The German State Railways had been developed since 1870 to meet Germany's strategic needs and under the command of Gen Rudolf Gercke they now performed miracles. On 10 and 11 December, for example, a daylight air raid on Koblenz railway yards, which were at the heart of the movement plan, left over 100 bomb craters in the yards, yet 24 hours later they were back in full operation. On 11 December, too, the main line to the Sixth SS Panzer Army's concentration area round Cologne and Euskirchen was severely damaged and all rail traffic halted. Next day trains were running normally. The Rhine rail bridges were reinforced; stores for repair were dumped beside them; 12 military bridges and 12 ferries were positioned to replace any bridges destroyed by air attack; trains moved by night or in bad weather; drivers' cabs were armoured; light anti-aircraft guns were mounted on all trains; and a tidal flow system was introduced on double track lines. Between 16 September and 15 December, 1,500 troop trains and 500 supply trains brought forward 12 armoured and 29 infantry divisions with 1,420 tanks and assault guns, together with 15,000 tons of ammunition and nearly five million gallons of motor fuel. By early

December this massive movement of troops, tanks and guns had drained the eastern front of most of its reinforcements and in the light of Russian claims to have contained the bulk of Germany's strength, it is interesting to note that the German tank strength on the eastern front in December 1944 was only 1,500, compared to 2,600 in the west.

There were still serious problems in the attacking armies. Spare parts for tanks, guns and vehicles were short. Many divisions lacked their proper scale of anti-tank guns. Motor transport was also inadequate and much of the artillery was still horse-drawn. Radios and telephone line equipment were deficient and in all divisions there were not enough engineers and bridging equipment. Even more decisive, as it turned out, was the weakness of the German Air Force. Only 800 aircraft were available instead of the 1,500 promised and they were only able to intervene effectively in the ground battle on one day.

Top: Mark IV tanks moving up by train, November 1944./*Bundesarchiv*

Above: Mark V Panther tanks being unloaded from flat-cars./*US Army*

Right: Portrait of an SS soldier./*US War Dept*

It soon became clear that the troops could not be in position to attack on 25 November and D-Day was postponed to 16 December. By the evening of the 15th all was ready. In the thick woods east of Monschau and Krewinkel the 1st SS Panzer Corps lay hidden. Their main punch consisted of two full strength and well trained divisions, the 1st SS Panzer (Leibstandarte) or 'Lifeguards', and the 12th SS Panzer (Hitlerjugend), backed up by the 3rd Parachute Division and the 12th and 277th Volksgrenadier or infantry divisions. East of the River Our and the high feature of the Schnee Eifel, the LVI Infantry Corps prepared to attack towards St Vith and to their south, Gen Walther Krueger's LVIII Panzer Corps and Gen Baron von Lüttwitz's XLVII Panzer Corps were to provide the Fifth Army's main effort. Although not given the recruiting and equipment priorities of the SS divisions, the army panzer divisions in these two corps – the 116th, 2nd and Panzer Lehr – were still well-equipped and experienced fighting units.

It was very cold and the villages, the high tree-covered hills, and deep valleys of the Ardennes were soon to be covered in snow. Three German armies had marched through the Ardennes in 1914 and three more in 1940, with the rumble of tanks replacing the jingling trot of von Richtofen's cavalry. Now rain and mist prevented the Allied air forces from flying and the German troops moved up unseen to their start lines. A few staff officers at American headquarters warned of something brewing in the Ardennes, but their views were disregarded and the Allies pressed on with their plans to defeat Germany, undisturbed by any idea of a major German counter-attack.

2 The Allied Positions

By mid-December 1944 the Allied armies were closing up to the German borders and, although the pace of their advance had slowed after the exhilarating thrusts across France and into Belgium and Holland in the late summer and autumn, Allied commanders were confident, that the end of the war was in sight.

In the north, Field Marshal Montgomery's 21st Army Group, with the First Canadian, Second British and Ninth United States Armies under his command, had reached the Rivers Maas and Roer. In Gen Omar Bradley's 12th Army Group, the United States First Army had closed up to the West Wall or Siegfried Line from Aachen to Luxembourg, while Gen George Patton's Third United States Army had fought through the Vosges Mountains to

Lt-Gen Courtney H. Hodges, commanding the US First Army. /US Army

the banks of the Rhine. South of Strasbourg the United States Seventh Army and the French First Army were also driving for the Rhine.

The front extended from the sea to the Swiss frontier. It was impossible to be strong everywhere, if forces were to be concentrated in sufficient strength to break through the Germans' final defence lines, to cross their last ditch, the River Rhine, and to invade Germany itself. In the US First Army Lt-Gen Courtney Hodges had deliberately thinned out his forces holding the Ardennes, in order to provide enough strength to drive through south of Aachen to capture the River Roer dams and to prevent the Germans from flooding the US First and Ninth Armies' line of advance into Germany.

In the north of the Ardennes Maj-Gen Leonard Gerow's V Corps held the front with four infantry divisions, two armoured combat commands and a cavalry group. A combat command was about a third of an armoured division and a cavalry group in the US Army was a reconnaissance battalion, mounted in light tanks and armoured cars. The southern part of this sector from Monschau to Buchholz was held by the 99th Infantry Division and through the left of this division, two more United States divisions, the 2nd and the 78th, were attacking towards the Roer dams on 16 December.

The centre of the Ardennes was held by the US VIII Corps, commanded by Maj-Gen Troy Middleton. On his north flank the 14th Cavalry Group covered a four-mile gap between the 99th Division and his 106th Infantry Division by a screen of mobile patrols, based on small garrisons in each village. The 106th Division had just arrived from the United States and was new to action. The general, Alan Jones, a quiet, methodical and conscientious commander, was unhappy about the fact that two of his regiments, the 422nd and the 423rd Infantry, had taken over positions well forward on the crests of the mountainous feature, the Schnee Eifel. His third regiment, the 424th, held positions somewhat to the south and west of the Schnee Eifel with a gap between them and the 423rd, covered by a reconnaissance troop. The whole division was responsible for more than 21 miles of front, including the Losheim gap in the north watched by the 14th Cavalry.

South of the 106th Division the 28th Infantry Division were dug in along the River Our. Both the 28th and the 4th Division on their right had seen much hard fighting and had played a distinguished part in the battles of the Hürtgen Forest in October and November. Casualties had been severe and they were now in this quiet sector of the Ardennes, absorbing and training 9,000 reinforcements. Like the 106th, the 28th Division were spread over a wide front from Lützkampen in the North to Wallendorf in the South, a distance of 20 miles, and the only reserve in the hand of Maj-Gen Norman 'Dutch' Cota was one battalion of his centre regiment, the 110th Infantry. Next in line to the south was the 4th

Above: Maj-Gen Norman D. Cota, commanding the 28th Division accepts some home-made cookies from Sergeant Joseph Bunch of the 110th Infantry./*US Army*

Above left: The US 28th Infantry Division are welcomed by the people of Bastogne, as they arrive there in September 1944./*US Army*

Left: 28th Division infantry with flame-throwers and tank support, advancing east of Bastogne in September 1944./*US Army*

Infantry Division on the flank of VIII Corps and on their right was a narrow sector held by a combat command of the 9th Armored Division, another unit new to battle.

Gen Middleton's VIII Corps headquarters was at Bastogne, the key road centre in the southern part of the Ardennes. He himself had fought in World War I and in Sicily, Normandy and Brittany, establishing a reputation for coolness and sound tactical leadership. V Corps headquarters was at Eupen and Gen Hodges' First Army command post was at Spa. Their overall commander, Gen Bradley, had his 12th Army Group headquarters some way to the south in Luxembourg city.

So on a front of about 50 miles four American divisions, the 99th, 106th, 28th, and 4th – reinforced by part of the 9th Armored Division and the 14th Cavalry Group – were unaware that 30 German panzer, panzer grenadier and infantry divisions were hidden in the woods a few miles to the east and were about to launch a full scale attack on them.

The reasons for this failure to spot so large an enemy concentration or to estimate more accurately German strengths and intentions have been discussed in detail ever since. There was certainly a mood of optimism amongst the Allies. They expected, too, a rational reaction from the new German Commander in Chief West, von Rundstedt, expecting him to conduct an orderly, fighting withdrawal to the Rhine. The Allies had not realised the degree to which Hitler was still controlling policy and strategy and had underestimated the remaining German military and industrial strength. In spite of 1914 and 1940, the Ardennes was still regarded as unsuitable country for large scale operations and the eyes of the Allied commanders, their air reconnaissance, had been blinded for some days by bad weather.

Some reports of unusual activity did reach American commanders. Both the 28th and 106th Divisions reported hearing the noise of vehicles and tank tracks between 13 and 15 December, but this was considered a normal relief of units in the line. On 14 December a woman refugee came into the 28th Division headquarters and reported that the woods near Bitburg were crammed with German troops and guns. She was sent on to Corps and Army headquarters, but only reached the latter at Spa on 16 December.

Then in the evening of 15 December four German prisoners, two of them wounded, and two deserters, told of a major attack coming in a day or two, but the deserters were thought to be unreliable and the wounded men were under morphine. Little notice was taken of their reports, since they were typical of many others which had proved to be baseless.

3 The Weapons

By late 1944 the American armoured units and many of the British too were equipped with the M4A2 Sherman tank. In its third year of service the 30ton Sherman with its 425hp Chrysler petrol engine was a reliable, well designed tank. Its short-barrelled 75mm gun was now outmatched by the German tank guns, but a few Shermans were becoming available in each tank battalion, armed with a new long-barrelled 76mm gun. The 'Jumbo' Sherman with heavier armour was also available in small numbers.

Pitted against the Sherman were three German tanks. The Mark IV, originally used in the May 1940 campaign, had now been developed into a reliable tank with a 268hp Maybach diesel engine, two 7.92mm machine guns and a 75mm gun, equal to the new American 76mm. About 27 tons in weight, the Mark IV, like the Sherman, could do 25mph, on roads. There were 800 of them in the divisions of the Sixth and Fifth Panzer Armies. There were also 750 Mark V Panthers, a fine-looking tank, weighing 50 tons and with its 594hp Maybach diesel engine, capable of 34mph. It had a very effective 75mm high velocity gun and good, thick armour, but it was still suffering from mechanical teething troubles.

In answer to the Russian heavy tank the Germans had produced the Mark VI Tiger, only four tons heavier than the Panther, but with up to two more inches of armour and carrying an 88mm gun – a real killer. 250 of these tanks were available for the Ardennes offensive. An even larger version, the 69ton King Tiger, had been produced, but only very few were in action by the end of 1944.

The Allied tank crews had already proved the ability of the Sherman to take on the Mark IV on equal terms, but to defeat a Mark V Panther, a Sherman had to manoeuvre to get a shot at the German's flank or rear. If a Tiger appeared, only a lucky shot from a Sherman against a track sprocket or on the turret ring would prevent the brewing up of the Sherman. This characteristic of bursting into flames, when hit, deriving from its petrol engine, was the origin of the German nick-name for the Sherman – the 'Ronson' tank.

Both sides fought with similar field and medium artillery. In the US Army the self-propelled 105mm howitzers of the armoured divisions on their tracked chassis proved their value in moving rapidly into action, whenever fire was needed in this fast moving battle and in the later stages the VT or proximity fuzes of their shells added to their fire effect. This fuze was a British invention, which exploded the shell at a set height before impact, showering troops in the open or in slit trenches without head cover with a lethal hail of steel fragments.

Below: An M4A3 Sherman, armed with a 76mm main gun, of the US 4th Armored Division near Bastogne on 8 January 1945./*US Army*

Above left: Mark IV on the road in Belgium.
/*Bundesarchiv*

Centre left: Replacing a Mark IV's track.
/*Bundesarchiv*

Below: A Mark V Panther tank advancing.
/*Bundesarchiv*

Above left: Mark V Panther crews at maintenance./*Bundesarchiv*

Centre left: A Mark VI Tiger tank with one track off. Behind it is a Volkswagen staff car. /*Bundesarchiv*

Below: King Tiger./*Bundesarchiv*

A series of photographs showing the crew of a Mark VI Tiger: *Left:* the tank commander; *Below left:* the radio operator; *Below centre:* the loader and gun-layer; *Below:* the driver. /*All Bundesarchiv*

Bottom: Effect on a Sherman tank of the German 88mm armour-piercing shell./*IWM*

CONCERTO IN C

The Germans had copied the Russians in producing large numbers of rocket launchers or Minenwerfer, known to Allied troops as 'Moaning Minnies'. They were light, easy to manufacture and although inaccurate, they put down a lot of high explosive. The 150mm 'Werfer' fired off $\frac{1}{4}$ton of explosive in 10 seconds and the bigger 210mm version fired $\frac{1}{2}$ton in one salvo. This flood of rockets arrived with a weird, moaning shriek and burst with tremendous blast and concussion.

For fighting against tanks the infantry of both sides used a hand-launched rocket, the American bazooka and the German Panzerfaust. Both had to be fired within 10 to 20 yards of a tank to be sure of a hit and it took a brave man to do it. The Americans also had the British six-pounder or 57mm anti-tank gun, now becoming obsolete, as the shells would bounce off a Panther or a Tiger. The bigger, towed, three-inch anti-tank gun was often effective, particularly against the German Mark IV tank, but the crew's lack of mobility and protection led to heavy casualties.

On both sides the self-propelled, tracked anti-tank gun played a decisive role. On many occasions the American M10 tank destroyer with its 90mm gun knocked out all three types of German tank, while the German 75mm and 88mm assault guns, as they called them, played a major part in all their battles.

Both sides used much the same anti-aircraft guns – 88mm and 90mm heavy anti-aircraft guns, 40mm Bofors and 20mm Oerlikons,

but only the Americans were equipped with the 'Quad .50s'. This was a quadruple mounting of .50 cal machine guns on a half-track vehicle and was capable of a high rate of fire. There were few Luftwaffe targets, but the Americans used them effectively as a mobile reserve of fire-power against ground targets, bringing them forward whenever a position was threatened by enemy attack.

Rifles, pistols, grenades, machine guns and mortars were roughly of equivalent effectiveness on both sides and the only significantly superior hand-weapon was the German machine pistol, the Schmeisser. This reliable and well made weapon was issued in large numbers to every type of unit and was particularly effective at the close ranges of village and woodland fighting.

Left: German rocket launchers firing./*IWM*

Below left: American bazooka being fired by men of the US 53rd Tank Battalion, 4th Armored Division – part of their training before joining their unit in Belgium; January 1945./*US Army*

Right: German infantry on the march in December 1944. The first man carries a Panzerfaust and the second man a Machine Gun 42, for which they are all carrying spare ammunition belts./*IWM*

Below: American gunners moving the British built 6pdr or 57mm anti-tank gun./*IWM*

Top left: American 90mm, being used near Stavelot in an anti-tank role by men of the US 30th Division, January 1945./*US Army*

Bottom left: The American quadruple .50cal machine gun the famous 'quad 50s'./*US Army*

Top right: German 88mm anti-aircraft gun./*IWM*

Centre right: The Geman MG42 in a bunker position./*Bundesarchiv*

Below: The German Schmeisser machine carbine in action./*Bundesarchiv*

Below right: The German infantry gun, a close support weapon, used well forward within the infantry battalion./*Bundesarchiv*

4 The Sixth SS Panzer Army Attacks

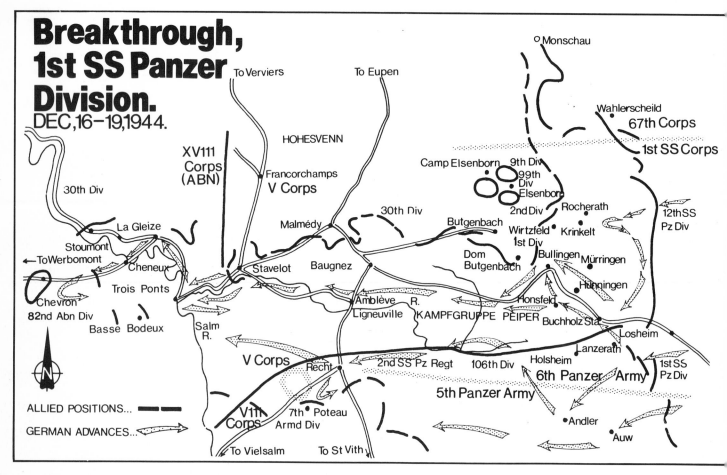

Breakthrough, 1st SS Panzer Division.
DEC,16–19,1944.

To Verviers

To Eupen

○ Monschau

HOHESVENN

Wahlerscheild

67th Corps

1st SS Corps

XV111 Corps (ABN)

Francorchamps
V Corps

Camp Elsenborn 9th Div

99th Div Elsenborn

12th SS Pz Div

30th Div

30th Div

Malmédy

2nd Div Rocherath

La Gleize

Butgenbach

Wirtzfeld • Krinkelt
1st Div

Stoumont

←To Werbomont

Cheneux

Stavelot   Baugnez

Dom Butgenbach

Bullingen Mürringen

Trois Ponts

Hünningen

Chevron

Amblève R.

Honsfeld

82nd Abn Div

Ligneuville

KAMPFGRUPPE PEIPER

Buchholz Sta

Basse Bodeux

Salm R.

Losheim

Lanzerath

V Corps

Recht

2nd SS Pz Regt

106th Div

Holsheim

Holsheim 6th Panzer Army

1st SS Pz Div

5th Panzer Army

V111 Corps

7th Armd Div

• Poteau

• Andler

Auw

To Vielsalm

To St Vith

ALLIED POSITIONS... ▬ ▬

GERMAN ADVANCES... ⇨

N

Above: Breakthrough by the 1st SS Panzer Division

Left: A drawing by Harrison Standley, the American war artist, of Hofen, held by the 3rd Battalion, 39th Infantry, 99th Division, just south of Monschau./*US Army*

Above right: German infantry advancing past a burning US jeep./*IWM*

Right: A US command post in the Monschau forest./*US Army*

The main punch of the Sixth SS Panzer Army was to be delivered by the 1st SS Panzer Corps. Gen Hermann Priess ordered his three infantry divisions, the 12th and 277th Volksgrenadier and the 3rd Parachute, to break into the American defences and open the way for his two SS panzer divisions to start their dash for the Meuse. On the right flank of this hole in the American line, Gen Otto Hitzfeld's LXVIII Corps would assault each side of Monschau and then dig in, facing northwards to form a hard shoulder for the armoured break-out.

At 5.30am on 16 December the German guns, rocket launchers and mortars opened fire all along the front and continued an intense bombardment of the American positions for an hour and a half. This was the heaviest artillery barrage fired by the Germans in the whole North-West Europe campaign. The weight and fury of the fire took the Americans by surprise and in the 394th Infantry of the 99th Division, where the German artillery against them had been estimated at two horse-drawn battalions, an officer exclaimed 'they're sure working those horses to death'.

All through the day the German infantry of the 12th and 277th Divisions struggled with the US 99th Division, suffering heavy casualties but making some inroads and causing General Lauer to throw in his last reserves. The Germans at Monschau in the north were thrown back with terrible losses but in the Losheim Gap, between the US 99th and 106th Divisions, thinly held by the US 14th Cavalry, the German 3rd Parachute Division broke through to Lanzerath. Although the American cavalry screen disintegrated and there was little to stop the German parachute infantry, they were slow to advance and by night-fall had still not cleared the way for the leading tanks of the 1st SS Panzer Division.

These were the Mark V Panthers and Mark IVs of Battlegroup Peiper, a force of tanks, infantry, guns and engineers, formed from the 1st SS Panzer Regiment as a nucleus, and led by Obersturm-

Top: SS armour pass a ditched American half-track, as Peiper's battlegroup advances./*IWM*

Above left: Obersturmbannführer or SS Lt-Col Jochen Peiper. /*Bundesarchiv*

Above right: Men of the 3rd Parachute Division on one of Peiper's tanks, 17 December 1944./*Bundesarchiv*

bannführer, or SS Col Jochen Peiper. Peiper was an ardent Nazi with a great reputation as a tank leader. He had won his first Iron Cross in Poland and had fought in Holland, France, the Balkans and Russia, where he added the Knight's Cross to his decorations. By November 1943 he was in command of the 1st SS Panzer Regiment and had been awarded the Oakleaves to his Knight's Cross. He and his battlegroup had been waiting all day for the 12th Volksgrenadier Division to open a road for him through the

US 99th Division and had been delayed in moving forward by the long columns of horse-drawn transport and artillery in front of him. Now at 7.30pm he was ordered to swing south and west through the 3rd Parachute Division. On reaching Lanzerath he was infuriated by the failure of the parachute officers to press on and their exaggeration of the enemy strength ahead. Ordering a parachute battalion to climb onto his vehicles, he drove on westwards in his Volkswagen with his driver, Zwigert. At midnight he struck at Buchholz, overrunning two platoons of the American 3rd Battalion 394th Infantry. Only one man escaped, a company radio operator in the command post cellar near the station, and for the next few hours he kept in touch with his battalion headquarters, reporting Germans in the rooms above and then the movement westwards of 30 German tanks and 28 half-tracks, full of infantry, with columns of men marching by on foot.

By 5am on 17 December the road from Buchholz to Honsfeld was packed with American vehicles of all kinds moving westwards, ahead of the German advance, and Peiper's tanks simply joined in the stream of traffic. The few American troops in Honsfeld, two platoons of the 801st Tank Destroyer Battalion, some anti-aircraft guns and a cavalry troop were taken by surprise and overwhelmed in a few minutes. The route for the 1st SS Panzer Division had been laid down as being Lanzerath-Buchholz-Honsfeld-Schoppen, but as the road to Schoppen was only a rough track, Peiper now turned north onto the better road westwards through Bullingen. This had been assigned to the 12th SS Panzer Division, but as they were still held up miles to the east, Peiper decided to 'borrow' their route for a few miles. The American 254th Engineers and some anti-tank gunners were badly mauled and thrown out of Bullingen by 7am, where Peiper found a fuel dump and refuelled

Top left: More German parachute soldiers on a tank of Peiper's battlegroup from the 1st SS Panzer Division, 17 December 1944. /*US Army*

Top right: German soldiers by a wrecked US half-track./*IWM*

Above: Drawing by Harrison Standley, American war artist, of Dom Butgenbach, where the US 26th Infantry of the 1st Division held the 1st SS Panzer Division's attacks. 500 German dead were found in the woods to the left of the drawing after the battle./*US Army*

his tanks, using American prisoners to do the work. The roads to the west of Peiper's battlegroup were clear, except for a mass of American trucks and jeeps escaping to the west, but the US 1st Division, the 'Big Red One', had now been ordered forward to reinforce the 2nd and 99th Divisions at this northern shoulder of the bulge. By this time on the morning of 17 December the 26th

Above right: More parachute soldiers on a Panther tank, near Bullingen, 17 December 1944./*US Army*

Right: A knocked out German tank and a US M10 in the 26th infantry positions at Butgenbach./*US Army*

Below: German prisoners, taken by the US 1st Division – some SS, some infantry and some air force./*US Army*

Above left: A German fuel convoy on fire after attack by US 8th Air Force fighter-bombers./*US Air Force*

Above: A Luftwaffe pilot bales out, after his aircraft is hit by machine gun fire from Major James Dalglish's fighter of the US 354th Group./*US Air Force*

Left, below left and below: Peiper, his driver Zwigert and two of his men at a crossroads west of Honsfeldt on 17 December 1944. /*US Army*

Above: The abandoned and shot-up vehicles of Battery B./*US Army*

Left: Henri Le Joly, a witness to the massacre./*US Army*

Above right: The field, in which the American prisoners were lined up – their bodies still covered in snow./*US Army*

Right: The tragedy is revealed./*US Army*

Infantry were arriving at Butgenbach and Bullingen and the US 7th Armored Division was also on the move towards St Vith from its harbour area 15 miles north of Aachen. Its two main columns of tanks and vehicles were now approaching Peiper's route forward, but these two groups of US and German tanks were unaware of the other's presence.

As Peiper left Bullingen, the skies cleared and two squadrons of American fighter-bombers, the 366th and 389th dived onto his column, setting fire to several vehicles, while above them their top cover, the fighters of 390th Squadron, jettisoned their bombs and engaged a flock of Bf109s, shooting down seven of them. Peiper drove on, by now in a captured jeep, close up behind his leading tanks and on reaching the Baugnez crossroads, bumped into the trucks and jeeps of a small American unit, moving towards St Vith. This was Battery B of the 285th Field Artillery Observation

Battalion, a unit whose function was to provide forward observers and communications for the control of artillery fire and who were armed only with rifles and machine guns. In minutes a few rounds of tank fire had set their vehicles ablaze and the German tanks were moving on westwards, leaving to the troops behind the job of rounding up the prisoners.

Only a few minutes before a combat command of the US 7th Armored Division had crossed Peiper's route at the same crossroads, heading south.

The American prisoners were now collected and marched into a field near the crossroads, where about 100 of them stood chatting in a group. A farmer, Henri Lejoly, watched them from the door of the roadside café and then turned to look, as more of Peiper's men came rattling down the road in half-tracks. In one of them, a private soldier, Georg Fleps, a 'Volksdeutscher' or ethnic German from the German mediaeval settlements in Romania, lifted his pistol and fired twice at the group of Americans. His first shot hit a soldier standing beside 2-Lt Virgil Larry, who was to survive the massacre, and the man fell down with blood running from a chest wound. Then machine guns opened fire from other German vehicles on the road and the American prisoners began to go down amid a chorus of shouts and cries. Some began crawling away, a few feigned dead, waiting breathlessly, as two or three Germans walked among the dead and wounded, finishing off with their pistols those, who they thought were alive. In fact some 20 of them survived and an hour later they got to their feet and ran for the nearby wood. Some were shot down, but several escaped and were picked up that afternoon by a patrol from the American 291st Engineers led by Lt-Col Peregrin. The news of this massacre spread rapidly and had reached Headquarters First Army four hours later and most of the troops in the area by that night. As usual with terror tactics, the effect rebounded onto the perpetrators and the chances of an SS soldier being taken prisoner in the days to come were sharply reduced. It transpired later that the Peiper battlegroup had already shot 19 unarmed American prisoners of war at Hons-

feld and most of the 50 at Bullingen after they had been made to refuel the SS tanks, and in the next three days they were to bring their total such killings to 350 Americans and 100 Belgian civilians. At the war crime trials in 1946 Sepp Dietrich, commander of the Sixth SS Panzer Army, confirmed that he had followed Hitler's directive in issuing an Army order 'to show no human inhibitions' and many of the SS in the 1st SS Panzer Division had fought in the brutal conditions of the Russian front. Peiper himself had been Himmler's adjutant and was probably imbued with his ruthless disregard for human life. It is also true that many German Army and Waffen SS officers were disgusted by these massacres and in several cases intervened to stop them.

After the war over 1,100 men of the 1st SS Panzer Division were questioned in the search for the men responsible for these massacres. 74 were finally brought to trial by the US Army at Dachau on 16 May 1946, including Sepp Dietrich, Fritz Kraemer, Priess, Jochen Peiper, his company commanders and senior NCOs, and several private soldiers with Peiper's driver Zwigert amongst them. The defence was conducted by seven German lawyers, led by Lt-Col Willis Everett, and was based on the claim, that the statements and confessions of the accused had been obtained under duress. On 16 July 1946, 43 were condemned to death and 22 to life imprisonment. Peiper and Fleps, who had fired the first shot, were amongst those sentenced to be hanged. A series of appeals and reviews followed, Lt-Col Everett spent 10 years and large sums of money in their defence and finally all the death sentences were quashed. In February 1951 most of the prisoners were released, Dietrich's release followed in 1955 and Peiper was set free in December 1956. He was still only 43, but he faced a difficult future. Firms were reluctant to employ him, he was involved in

Right: Belgian civilians killed at Stavelot. /*IWM*

Below: German soldiers amid abandoned American tents and equipment. /*US Army*

Below right: SS men of Peiper's battlegroup advancing over a rough track./*IWM*

further war crimes investigations in Italy in 1946, and in 1977 he was murdered in France, probably by the Baader-Meinhof gang.

Not all the killing of civilians was done by the German SS units. Little research has been done into the part played by the Belgian Maquis in the battle, but it seems probable that a number of murders were carried out by Maquisards. The German speaking part of the Ardennes around St Vith and along the eastern frontier of Belgium and Luxembourg was part of Germany up to 1918 and many of the inhabitants were still German in culture, background and sentiment. Lt-Gen Desobry, who as a major commanded the garrison of Noville in their stand against the 2nd Panzer Division, certainly believed that the Noville schoolmaster, M. Lutgen, was shot by the Maquis and Maj-Gen Wegener, Chief of Staff in the 5th Panzer Army, still thinks that the field hospital of the 101st Airborne Division at Herbaimont was captured by Maquis, rather than by advanced elements of 2nd Panzer Division.

By 1pm that same day, 17 December, Peiper's men reached Ligneuville, where they saw American supply trucks of the 9th Armored Division trying to get away at the other end of the village. The Germans accelerated, but a single Sherman, immobilised near the village hotel with one track off for repair, opened fire and knocked out the leading armoured car. A Tiger tank replied with its 88mm and the Sherman flamed. As the light failed that evening, Peiper's tanks reached the high ground east of the river bridge at Stavelot, where they were fired on by a bazooka from a road block set up by the 291st Engineers. The crews could see that the town and the roads across the river were jammed with American vehicles. These were in fact, part of the 7th Armored Division moving south and supply trucks moving north to clear the huge First Army fuel dump of 2½ million gallons only four miles away at Francorchamps. Peiper's orders and aim were to drive on through Stavelot, Trois Ponts, Werbomont, Oufet and Seny to Huy on the Meuse, another 50 miles on, but now his column halted for the night, east of the undefended Stavelot bridge and unaware of the precious fuel dump so close to their north, a surprising departure from Peiper's normal, driving leadership. Unknown to him, the only combat troops in Stavelot that evening were 13 men of the 291st Engineers, but during the night a battalion of the 526th Armored Infantry from the 3rd Armored Division reached the town and worked furiously to prepare their defences for the next day's battle.

5 The Northern Shoulder Holds

Above: The 26th Infantry of the 1st Division moving up to Bullingen. /*US Army*

Left: A gunner, Leon Willett, emerges from his dug-out in the gun-lines of the 2nd Division./*US Army*

While the 1st SS Panzer Division was thrusting westwards, followed by the 3rd Parachute Division, having burst through the Losheim gap between the American V and VIII Corps, German infantry were hammering at the American 99th Division, trying to break open the road westwards for the 12th SS Panzer Division. By that first evening of 16 December the 99th were hard pressed and the US 1st Infantry Division were moving down to their aid. To add to the confusion, the US 2nd Division was still attacking north-west towards Wahlerscheid, on the left of the US 99th Division, while the Germans were pressing in on the right. The American 394th Infantry were finally driven out of Losheimergraben and the Germans pushed on to attack the next village to the west, Hünningen, held by the 1st Battalion, 23rd Infantry, part of the US 2nd Division. Gen Gerow, V Corps commander, now asked First Army for permission to break off the 2nd Division attack and

to pull back five miles to the strong, natural defensive position of the Elsenborn ridge. This was refused, as the German attack further south was still not recognised for what it was – an all out offensive by three armies. The 2nd Division, however, began to move its reserve battalions into the twin villages of Rocherath-Krinkelt, through which the bulk of the 2nd Division and the remnants of the 99th would have to withdraw.

For the next two days the battle raged for these two villages. The Germans fought to open the roads for the 12th SS Panzer Division and the Americans to defend the routes back to their chosen positions on the Elsenborn ridge. Tanks from the SS joined in to support the infantry of the German 12th and 277th Divisions, the losses mounted on both sides and much of the US 99th Division's guns and vehicles were abandoned, as the roads to their widely spread battalions were cut. But the green troops of the US 99th and the more experienced men of the 2nd Division fought well from their fox-holes in the snow, crouching down to let the German tanks roll over them and then getting up again to shoot down the German infantry. Sgt Vernon McGarity in the 393rd Infantry, east of Rocherath, won the Medal of Honor, knocking

Above left: The gun-lines of the 38th Field Artillery Battalion, 2nd Division, in action on 20 December./*US Army*

Left: Company A, 38th Infantry, move forwards to Krinkelt on 17 December./*US Army*

Above: A German crew-man comes away from a burning Panther, 17 December./*US Army*

Right: Men of the 23rd Infantry blowing fox-holes in the frozen ground. /*US Army*

Below: An engineer from the 2nd Division laying anti-tank mines. /*US Army*

out German tanks with his bazooka, while in the 9th Infantry withdrawing towards Rocherath from the north, Pvt William Soderman won the same precious award by stopping three German tanks with bazooka rounds, although badly wounded by machine gun fire. In the 1st Battalion 23rd Infantry, hurriedly moved forward to positions just east of Krinkelt, the left flank company gave way under a heavy German attack by tanks and infantry and Pvt Richard Cowan won the Medal of Honor by a gallant attempt to cover his company's retreat.

On 18 December Gen Priess, commanding the 1st SS Panzer Corps, determined to take Rocherath and Krinkelt. He threw into the attack the complete 989th Grenadier Regiment of the 277th Volksgrenadier Division, the 25th Panzer Grenadier Regiment of the 12th SS Panzer Division, an assault gun battalion and two tank battalions of Tigers and Panthers – a total of six infantry and three armoured battalions. Holding the villages were the three US battalions of the 38th Infantry, a good deal reduced in strength, half the 9th Infantry, a few platoons of the 23rd, the 741st Tank Battalion and some tank destroyers from the 644th, 612nd and 801st Battalions. Perhaps more importantly the bulk of the 2nd and 99th Division artillery were now in position on the Elsenborn ridge, five miles to the west, with their observers forward in the front line, all ready to give effective fire support.

The Germans attacked early in the morning of 18 December and fierce fighting went on all day in the two villages. Tanks and infantry milled around the houses, blazing away at point blank range; the American artillery pounded each German attack as it came in; several American companies were over-run and wiped out; but the defence held and the Germans fell back. Next day a fresh German division, the 3rd Panzer Grenadier, joined in the assault, but their two further attempts failed under a storm of

Left: William Soderman receives the Medal of Honor from President Truman on the White House lawn, 12 October 1945./*US Army*

Below: Drawing by Harrison Standley, the American war artist, of the crossroads in Rocherath./*US Army*

Right: Inside Krinkelt church after the battle./*US Army*

Below right: Gun position of the 38th Field Artillery near Elsenborn after intensive firing./*US Army*

Top left: Medium artillery firing from better camouflaged positions on the Elsenborn ridge. /*US Army*

Above left: An American L-19 Artillery observation aircraft, taking off to spot for the guns./*US Army*

Left: Survivors from the 1st Battalion, 395th Infantry, 99th Division./*US Army*

Above: A German lies dead in front of his knocked-out Panther tank./*US Army*

Right: A German prisoner of war at Bullingen. /*US Army*

American artillery fire. The 12th SS Panzer Division was now not only three days behind schedule in its planned dash for the Meuse, but had suffered heavy losses in men and tanks. They were now ordered to swing south, by-passing Krinkelt-Rocherath, to follow Peiper's route to the west. That evening the garrison of Krinkelt and Rocherath moved back to the Elsenborn ridge in an orderly withdrawal, covered by rearguards of tanks and tank destroyers and the US 99th, 2nd and 1st Divisions settled down to a stubborn defence of the northern shoulder of the Bulge, from which all attempts to shift them were to fail.

The US 99th and 2nd Divisions had lost 4,413 men, killed, wounded and missing and another 900 from trench feet and illness, but the German losses had been heavier and included 44 tanks.

Gen Preiss now moved his command post forward to Bullingen and for the next four days sent his armour and infantry into a series of fierce attacks at Butgenbach and Malmedy, trying to outflank the American defence and to widen the gap for his armoured divisions. All failed with heavy loss and the main effort now passed from Sepp Dietrich's Sixth SS Panzer Army to Von Manteuffel's Fifth Panzer Army further south.

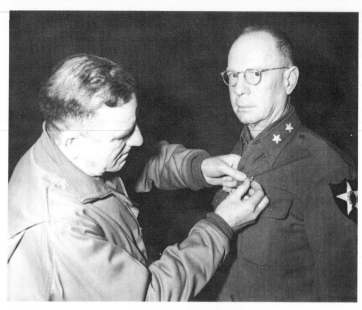

Top: Maj-Gen Leonard Gerow, commanding the US 1st Corps pins the Bronze Star on Maj-Gen William Robertson for his leadership of the 2nd Division./*US Army*

Above: The 3rd Battalion, 395th Infantry win the Presidential Citation for their part in the defence of the Northern shoulder./*US Army*

Left: Sgt George Talbert of the 2nd Battalion, 18th Infantry, 1st Division, on 19 December 1944, near Sourbrodt./*US Army*

6 The Fifth Panzer Army Destroys the US 106th Infantry Division

About eight miles east of the important road centre of St Vith lies the high wooded feature of the Schnee Eifel and across the top of it ran the Siegfreid Line from north east to south west. Two main roads ran west to St Vith through two valleys, the Losheim Gap just to the north of the Schnee Eifel and the valley of the river Alph to the south. Earlier American successes had taken their forward troops through the Siegfried Line on top of the Schnee Eifel and these positions were now held by two regiments of the US 106th Division. On the left was the 422nd Infantry, commanded by Col George Descheneaux and on the right the 423rd Infantry, led by Col Charles Lavender. The battalions had only arrived on the Schnee Eifel on 11 December and had taken over well prepared dug-outs and trenches, roofed with timber and many of them equipped with stoves, from the experienced and battle-tried 2nd Division. Between the 423rd Infantry and the 424th the Alph valley gap was covered by a cavalry squadron and beyond the 424th to the south was the US 28th Division.

It was a wide front and the infantry companies and platoons were strung out in a long line of defended posts. The division had been raised in March 1943, but had been milked of trained men several times to reinforce US divisions, hard hit in the Normandy fighting. They had never been in action before and now had only five days to get to know the country.

Gen Von Manteuffel gave to Gen Lucht and his LXVI Corps the task of seizing St Vith and its road net which would be essential for the German drive to the Meuse. Lucht had only two infantry divisions in his corps, the 18th and 62nd Volksgrenadiers. The 18th was already holding the line opposite the US 106th Division and knew the country fairly well. It had only formed in September from the remnants of an air force division and was made up of men

Below: Sgt Slashy and Pvt Phillips of the 424th Infantry roll up a sleeping bag./*US Army*

Left: Von Manteuffel talks to one of his Mark V tank crews./*Bundesarchiv*

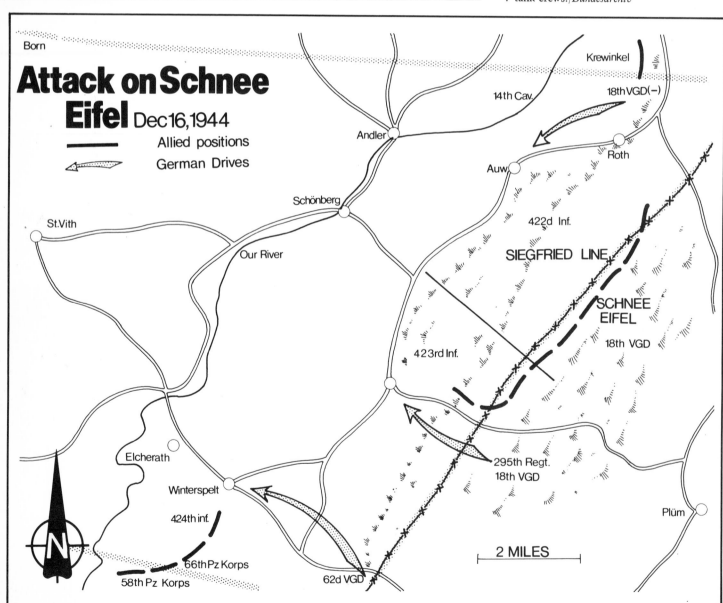

Attack on Schnee Eifel Dec 16, 1944

—— Allied positions

⇐ German Drives

Born

Krewinkel

14th Cav.

18th VGD(−)

Andler

Roth

Auw

Schönberg

422d Inf.

SIEGFRIED LINE

St. Vith

Our River

SCHNEE EIFEL

18th VGD

423rd Inf.

295th Regt.
18th VGD

Elcherath

Winterspelt

Plüm

424th inf.

N

66th Pz Korps

58th Pz Korps

62d VGD

2 MILES

Above: A German infantryman with machine gun belt, fighting knife and entrenching shovel./*IWM*

Above right: The same man with two mates and a captured US M8 armoured car behind them – probably from the US 14th Cavalry Group in the Losheim gap./*IWM*

Right: The same man again, this time smoking a captured American cigarette./*IWM*

from the air force and navy, hastily trained as infantrymen. The divisional commander, Gen Hoffmann-Schönborn was an experienced regular, but they were generally short of good leaders. However Lucht chose the 18th for the main assault on St Vith and directed them to put their main weight of attack round the north side of the Schnee Eifel through the Losheim gap, known to be lightly held by American reconnaissance patrols.

Lucht's second division, the 62nd, carried the number of a division destroyed on the Russian front and although fully equipped, was made up of raw reinforcements, new to battle. It only arrived in the Ardennes on 6 December, when Maj-Gen Frederick Kittel, its commander, was given orders to break through south of the Schnee Eifel and block the exits from St Vith to the south and west. Forty assault guns were to support both divisions, but they had no tanks and not much artillery.

At 4am on 16 December in the darkness of a frosty night the shock companies of the 18th Division began their advance. Relying on surprise and the wide gaps between the American positions in the Losheim gap and using no artillery, they were at Auw, two miles inside the American front line by 8.30am. By 11am the American 14th Cavalry Group had withdrawn to the Manderfeld ridge and by 4pm had been pushed back to Andler and Holzheim seven miles to the west. This left the northern flank of the 422nd Infantry dangerously exposed, as their supporting artillery regiments were in position round Auw and there were battalions well forward near Kobscheid and Schlausenbach. However, no serious attack on the 422nd Infantry occurred on that first day, as the two German regiments moving round their north flank were busy, driving back the 14th Cavalry Group.

At the south end of the 106th Division line, the 424th Infantry found itself under attack from the whole of the German 62nd Division. Heavy fighting went on all day with the Americans counter-attacking vigorously, but by the evening the Germans were

41

Left: German infantry moving through abandoned US positions on 17 December. /*US Army*

Below: German infantry run past a burning American vehicle. /*US Army*

Bottom: A German NCO waves on his section, while US vehicles burn on the road. /*US Army*

Right: German soldiers moving back along the same road. /*US Army*

in Winterspelt four miles into the American defences. Next day they attacked again and in spite of intense fire from the American artillery and the arrival of Combat Command B of the US 9th Armored Division with their Sherman tanks, the 424th Infantry were forced back behind the River Our.

The enemy were now closing a pair of pincers on the two American regiments on the Schnee Eifel. On the morning of 17 December, the second day of the battle, Gen Alan Jones telephoned his Corps commander, Gen Troy Middleton, at Bastogne on a bad line, which caused a serious misunderstanding. Both men were concerned about the 422nd and 423rd, but Middleton was reluctant to sanction a withdrawal and Jones perhaps gave Middleton too sanguine an impression. By now, the 14th Cavalry Group had pulled right back to the north-west of St Vith and the German 294th Grenadier Regiment had swung south to capture Schönberg, cutting the main road from the Schnee Eifel to St Vith. Another regiment of the 18th Division captured Bleialf in the early morning of the 17th and by 9am they had linked up with their sister regiment at Schönberg. The two American regiments on the Schnee Eifel were now surrounded. Of the two artillery regiments near Auw, the 592nd with its medium guns escaped the German net and got away to St Vith, but the 589th, attacked by German infantry in strength, destroyed its guns and scattered, while a third regiment in action nearer Schönberg moved east to the protection of the 423rd Infantry, but soon ran out of ammunition.

Above: German infantry advance across country./*IWM*

Left: A conference at Wiltz in November 1944. On the left Maj-Gen John Leonard of the 9th Armored Division, then Maj-Gen Troy Middleton, commanding the US VIII Corps; beside him Lt-Gen Omar Bradley, US, 12th Army Group and on the right Gen Eisenhower./*US Army*

The Schönberg road was a scene of complete confusion. Although the village was held now by Germans, a stream of American traffic was still trying to get through it to the west. A Volkswagen, full of German soldiers, pulled into an American column; a troop of American armoured cars going west overtook a German column on the same road and everyone was firing at everyone else. The Germans were now concentrating on moving their forces forward to capture St Vith and throughout the 17th made no attempt to attack the 9,000 Americans trapped on the Schnee Eifel. Late that night Gen Jones sent a message to his two regiments, telling them to break out to the west and promising an air drop of ammunition, food and water. The US troop carrier aircraft, back at Welford in England, loaded these supplies and flew out to Belgium, but a lack of coordination and drive led to the drop being cancelled.

Next day the two regimental commanders agreed to begin the move west at 10am, but from then onwards each regiment acted independently and with a steady deterioration in control. The 423rd tried to attack towards Schönberg, but was stopped by enemy fire. One battalion became separated from the regiment and was fired on in error by part of the 422nd and eventually the whole 423rd Infantry surrendered.

The 422nd came to a similar, sad end. In moving toward Schönberg the regiment lost the way and finally bivouacked in a wood, some miles east of Schönberg. At daybreak on the 19th the three battalions moved out once more and were just crossing the Bleialf-Auw road, when they were hit by tanks and infantry. This was the Führer Begleit Brigade, Hitler's Bodyguard, now formed into an independent tank brigade and moving up to help the 18th Division capture St Vith. At 2.30pm Col Descheneaux surrendered his brigade and some 8,000 Americans were marched away as prisoners of war.

Top: Harrison Standley's drawing of the crossroads on the Schönberg to Bleialf road – known as Purple Heart Corner./*US Army*

Below left: The Schönberg road, as seen by a US 9th Air Force reconnaissance pilot./*US Air Force*

Below: American prisoners of war./*US Army*

The Fifth Panzer Army Breaks Through the US 28th Division

While Gen Lucht's LXVI Corps was battering at the gates of St
Vith and capturing two thirds of the US 106th Division, the other
two corps of Manteuffel's Fifth Panzer Army were attacking the
US 28th Division further south, with the aim of making a rapid
breakthrough to the Meuse. On the north flank of this attack Gen
Walther Krueger's LVIII Panzer Corps planned to launch the
116th Panzer and 560th Volksgrenadier Divisions along the line
Duren–Houffalize–Namur and on their left Gen Baron von
Lüttwitz's XLVII Corps would drive through Dasburg and Clerf to
Bastogne and the Meuse, south of Namur, with the 2nd Panzer
and Panzer Lehr Divisions leading. Both Gen Krueger and Gen
von Lüttwitz were the personal choice of Field Marshal Model,
and were able leaders with a lot of experience in tank warfare.
Von Lüttwitz, in particular, belied his stocky, pompous appearance
by being a hard driving commander with a real understanding of
his profession and his men. In his XLVII Corps he had the famous
2nd Panzer Division and the Panzer Lehr Division, both of whom
had been in the thick of the fight since Normandy.

The 2nd Panzer had rested and re-equipped with 27 Mark IV
and 58 Mark V Panther tanks in the two battalions of the armoured
regiment. Some of these Panthers had the new, infra-red night
sight for their guns and generally the division was in good shape.
Their commander, Oberst Meinrad von Lauchert only reached
them on 15 December, but he too was Model's personal choice.
The Panzer Lehr Division, so named because of its origin as a
training and demonstration unit, had been a normal panzer
division since Normandy. Now it was short of men and only had

Above: Gen Heinrich Freiherr von Lüttwitz,
commanding the XLVII Panzer Corps.
/*Bundesarchiv*

Left: Oberst Meinrad von Lauchert,
commanding the 2nd Panzer Division.
/*Bundesarchiv*

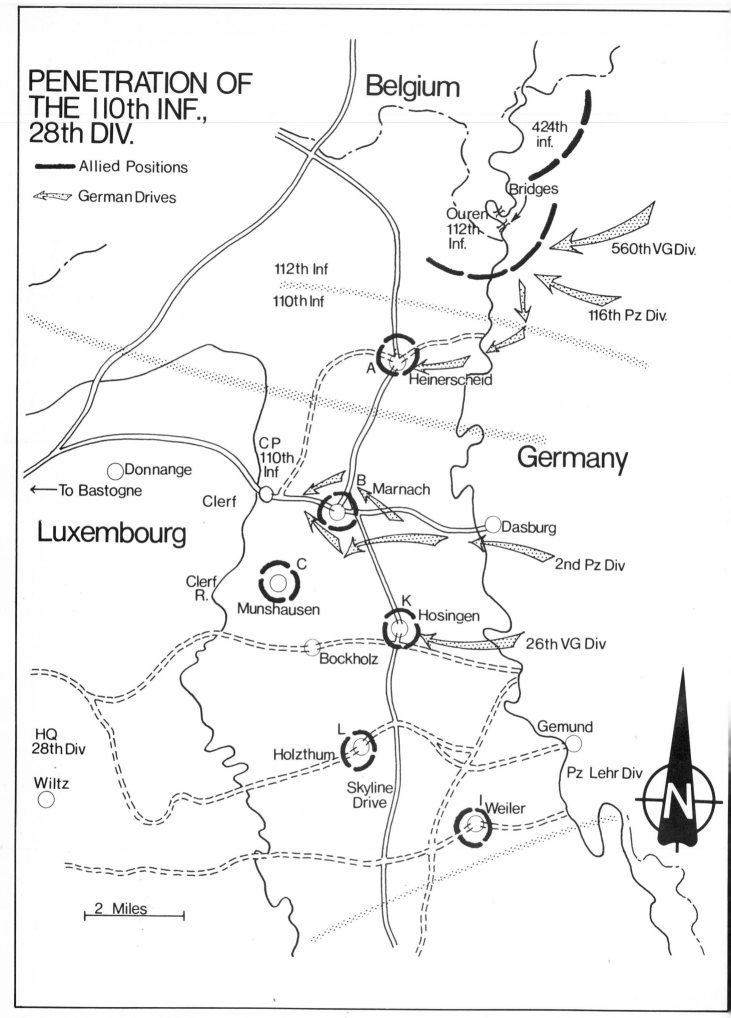

PENETRATION OF THE 110th INF., 28th DIV.

━━━ Allied Positions

⟨═══ German Drives

Belgium

424th inf.

Bridges

Ouren
112th Inf.

560th VG Div.

112th Inf
110th Inf

116th Pz Div.

A
Heinerscheid

Germany

C P
110th Inf

Donnange

To Bastogne

Clerf

B Marnach

Dasburg

Luxembourg

2nd Pz Div

Clerf R.

C

Munshausen

K
Hosingen

Bockholz

26th VG Div

HQ
28th Div

L

Holzthum

Gemund

Skyline Drive

Pz Lehr Div

Wiltz

I Weiler

N

2 Miles

Above: Maj-Gen Kokott, commanding the 26th Volksgrenadier Division. */Bundesarchiv*

Above right: Maj-Gen Siegfried von Waldenburg, commanding the 116th Panzer Division./*Bundesarchiv*

one tank battalion of 27 Mark IVs and 30 Mark Vs, instead of a full regiment. To make up for this deficiency the division was allotted four extra battalions of assault guns and a powerful, specially reinforced, reconnaissance battalion of tanks, armoured infantry and armoured cars. Their commander, Fritz Bayerlein, was the same age as the century. Another short, stocky general, he had fought against the British in World War I from the age of 16 and had served in the Western Desert continuously from October 1941 to May 1943, when he was wounded and flown back to Germany. For most of that time he was Field Marshal Rommel's Chief of Staff. He had been commanding his Panzer Lehr division since Normandy.

Von Lüttwitz's third division was the 26th Volksgrenadier, an old regular Army division, who had fought on the Russian front from July 1941 to the end of September 1944. Reformed at Poznan with reinforcements, mostly from the navy, it was now 17,000 strong, well equipped with modern weapons, but still relying on 5,000 horses for its transport. Gen Kokott and his remaining regular officers and NCO's had worked hard to make something

of their practically new division, although they did not consider their new title of *Volksgrenadier* much of an honour.

Gen Siegfried von Waldenburg's 116th Panzer Division had established a good, fighting reputation since June 1944 and although it had suffered heavy losses, the division now had 92 Mark V Panthers and 47 Mark IVs. The 560th Volksgrenadier Division was new to action, having spent all its life in Norway and included only two grenadier regiments under Gen Rudolph Langhäuser's command.

All these five German divisions, three panzer and two infantry, were now to hurl themselves against two American infantry regiments, the 112th and 110th of the US 28th Division, strung out over 20 miles between Lützkampen in the north and Weiler in the south. The 112th Infantry were holding the line with company strong-points in the villages just east of the River Our, covering two main road bridges at Ouren, while to their south the 110th Infantry were widely spaced along the main north-south road in the villages of Heinerscheid, Marnach, Münshausen, Hosingen, Holzthurm and Weiler. Col Harley Fuller's 110th Infantry command post was in the beautiful resort village of Clerf, two miles behind his forward companies.

At 5.30am the German guns and Minenwerfer opened fire, but the German infantry had already moved forward, closing up to the American positions without a preliminary barrage. Their assault came in, as their guns began. In the north both the 560th Volksgrenadier and the 116th Panzer Divisions met determined resistance and intense fire from the men of Col Nelson's 112th Infantry. Heavy losses in tanks and men piled up in front of Heckhuscheid and Berg and although some of the German infantry got into Harspelt, they were thrown out again by a vigorous counter-attack. Next day both German divisions attacked again, forcing the 112th Infantry to pull back a mile or two, but the German progress was so slow that the 116th Panzer Division were ordered to swing south

47

Above: The River Our between Luxembourg and Germany./*US Army*

Left: Driver and truck from the US 35th Combat Engineers, hit by German air attack near Heiderscheid in December 1944./*IWM*

Top right: Preparing anti-tank mines at an American company headquarters, 16 December./*IWM*

Right: American soldiers, killed near Hoscheiderdickt, probably in cold blood after capture./*US Army*

to follow through the wide gap made through the US 110th Infantry

Here the American infantry companies in their villages were surrounded almost at once on that first morning. Company I at Weiler was over-run by 6.30pm, Company K with some engineers at Hosingen held out until the morning of 18 December and at Marnach on the main route forward for the 2nd Panzer Division a fierce battle raged all day. Two companies of the 707th Tank Battalion were sent forward from Clerf by Col Fuller to reinforce his line and by nightfall it was still holding. Von Lüttwitz's bridges over the Our were now ready, however, and early on 17 December his tanks pressed on westwards, by-passing the Americans still holding out in Marnach and Hosingen.

Early that second morning Col Harley Fuller launched three converging counter-attacks to relieve Marnach – his reserve 2nd Battalion from Clerf; his Company C and a tank platoon from Münshausen and the 707th's light tanks from Heinerscheid in the north. They met the full strength of the 2nd Panzer Division and by that evening all the light tanks had been destroyed and the 2nd Battalion dispersed.

The Germans were by now already in Clerf. German tanks were

Above: Knocked out German half-tracks at Heiderscheid with some of their crews, lying dead beside them./*US Army*

Right: Wiltz, site of the command post of the US 28th Division. /*US Army*

Below right: German 20mm anti-aircraft gun in position above Wiltz. /*IWM*

firing at close range into Fuller's command post, the Claravallis Hotel. His headquarters company were besieged in the Chateau. Sherman tanks from Company A, 707th Tank Battalion, were fighting Mark IVs amongst the houses, knocking out four of them. Three Shermans were on fire. The 2nd Tank Battalion from Combat Command R, 9th Armored Division arrived to join in the fight, but by 6.30pm more German tanks and infantry were pouring into Clerf. Col Fuller and some of his staff climbed out of a back window of the hotel and escaped, only to be captured north-east of Wiltz two days later. The road to the west was open and the German 2nd Panzer Division drove on towards Bastogne and Noville, followed by the 116th Panzer Division, swinging north-west for Houffalize.

While the 2nd and 116th Panzers were crossing the Our river bridge at Dasburg all night on the 16th-17th, the Panzer Lehr Division began crossing at Gemund 10 miles to the south. On the 17th this division moved 10 miles to the west in the wake of the 26th Volksgrenadiers and by early morning on 18 December, Gen Bayerlein's powerful reconnaissance battalion had reached the outskirts of Wiltz.

Wiltz was the command post of the US 28th Division. In the town with Maj-Gen Norman Cota were Company G of the 110th Infantry, a few tanks of Combat Command R, 9th Armored Division, the 44th Combat Engineer Battalion, six 3-inch anti-tank guns, some gunners from the 687th Field Artillery and some anti-aircraft guns.

The 3rd Battalion of the 110th Infantry withdrew in good order from Weiler, Holzthum and Consthum, inflicting damage on the German 26th Division and eventually reaching Wiltz with some 200 men. Next day the bulk of the Panzer Lehr by-passed Wiltz, driving on for Bastogne and leaving Wiltz first to the 26th Volksgrenadier Division and then to the 5th Parachute Division. By midnight on 19 December the German infantry had fought their way into the town and the remnants of the garrison were cut to pieces, as they tried to escape to the west.

This was the end of the US 28th Division. The 112th Infantry had retreated to the north-west and had now joined the southern perimeter of the St Vith defences. The 109th Infantry had pivoted to the south joining with the 4th Infantry Division to form a firm southern shoulder to the bulge. The 110th Infantry had been destroyed, except for a few hundred men, who reached Bastogne and were there organised as an improvised reserve.

Above: Men from 28th Division band and quartermaster company, who escaped from Wiltz and reached Bastogne./*US Army*

Left: Maj-Gen Raymond Barton, commanding the US 4th Division with Gen Eisenhower in November 1944./*US Army*

Above: Men of the 4th Division supplement the rations, January 1945./*US Army*

Left: Pvts Adam Davis and Milford Sillars, survivors of the 110th Infantry in Bastogne on 19 December./*US Army*

Top right: Men of the 28th Division, reorganised in Bastogne as part of Team SNAFU, Gen McAuliffe's emergency reserve. /*US Army*

Above right: Crew of a 105mm self-propelled, tracked howitzer in action. This was the normal field artillery piece of the American armoured divisions./*US Army*

Right: An American 155mm shell landing on German bunkers across the Sauer river near Echternach./*US Army*

Five American tank companies and three engineer companies had also been lost, but it was now 20 December and the Fifth Panzer Army's timetable was already two days late.

On the southern flank of the 28th Division the German 5th Parachute Division and the 352nd Volksgrenadier Division attacked the 109th Infantry at the same time as the rest of the main offensive, as Gen Brandenberger's Seventh Army moved forward to form the southern flank of the German thrust to the Meuse. The 276th Volksgrenadiers drove into the American 60th Armored Infantry Battalion between Wallendorf and Bollendorf, and the 212nd attacked the US 12th Infantry in the 4th Division. After three days of fighting the American line held on the right, in spite of heavy odds against them, and when two combat teams from the 10th Armored Division arrived, the 109th Infantry, 9th Armored, 10th Armored and 4th Infantry Divisions dug in solidly on the line Echternach to Ettelbruck. Like the northern shoulder at Elsenborn, the southern shoulder held firm, while Gen Patton's Third Army prepared to attack the German salient from the south.

8 The Allies React

On the opening day of the German offensive, 16 December, Gen Eisenhower was at his headquarters near Paris, living in the villa which Field Marshal von Rundstedt had requisitioned for himself 18 months before. The day began quietly for the Supreme Allied Commander. A letter arrived from Field Marshal Montgomery, asking for leave to spend a day or two with his son in England; Ike's orderly, Micky McKeough married a WAC, Pearlie Hargrave; there was a presentation of Free Polish decorations to Ike and his Chief of Staff, Gen Walter Bedell Smith, and in the evening Gen Bradley, the Commanding General of 12th Army Group, arrived at 6pm to discuss with Ike the pressing problem of infantry reinforcements and to stay for a special dinner party.

This was something to which Gen Ike could look forward, since

Bradley was an old friend and his stay would relieve the loneliness of high command. During the evening brief by the staff on the battle situation, a message came in to Maj-Gen Kenneth Strong, the head of the SHAEF intelligence staff and he interrupted the briefing to tell Eisenhower and Bradley that the Germans had attacked the US V and VIII Corps that morning and had penetrated the front in five places. The most dangerous thrust seemed to be in the Losheim Gap on the Corps boundary. In the discussion which followed, Eisenhower made clear his belief that this was a major German offensive and he told Bradley to move two armoured divisions at once to the aid of Gen Middleton's VIII Corps. To the north in the Ninth Army the 7th Armored Division was out of the line and to the south Gen Patton had pulled back the

Left: A meeting at the US Ninth Army headquarters in Maastricht on 7 December 1944. From the left are Lt-Gen Omar Bradley, 12th Army Group; ACM Sir Arthur Tedder, Air Deputy to Gen Eisenhower; Gen Eisenhowever; Field Marshal Sir Bernard Montgomery, 21st Army Group and Lt-Gen William Simpson, US Ninth Army./*US Army*

Above: Maj-Gen Matthew Ridgway, commanding the US XVIII Airborne Corps and Maj-Gen James Gavin, 82nd Airborne Division at Remonchamps towards the end of the Ardennes battle. Ridgway is carrying the two grenades, which were his 'trade-mark' in action from Normandy right through to the end in Korea./*US Army*

Above right: Brig-Gen Antony McAuliffe, acting commander 101st Airborne Division, in Bastogne on 5 January./*US Army*

10th Armored Division to prepare for an attack in the Saar, due in three day's time. Bradley agreed, but reminded Ike how angry George Patton would be. 'Tell him Ike is running this damn war', was the reply. These orders were sent out at once and although Patton argued fiercely against losing his reserve armoured division, once a firm order was given he got his troops moving with his usual efficiency and speed.

The only other reserve divisions in Europe were the American 82nd and 101st Airborne Divisions, refitting near Rheims after their battles in Holland. In England there were three more US divisions, the 17th Airborne, the 87th Infantry and the 11th Armored, all new to combat, and the British 6th Airborne Division. After five years of war British man-power was running out and any major reinforcements which the Allies might need for the rest of the war, would have to come from the USA.

That same evening Gen Hodges at First Army released the US 1st Infantry Division, the Big Red One, to Gen Gerow at V Corps. They marched south the same night to strengthen the northern shoulder and took up positions west of the 99th and 2nd Divisions, just in time to block the 12th SS Panzer Division.

As the German 1st SS Panzer Corps continued their attempt to widen the breach in the American lines and to outflank the Ameri-

can hold on the Elsenborn Ridge, it became urgently necessary to prolong the V Corps line to the west. On 17 December, therefore, Gen Gerow ordered the 30th Infantry Division to move south to Malmedy and Stavelot and they too arrived in time to stop Jochen Peiper's battlegroup of the 1st SS Panzer Division, as he struggled to find a way through to the Meuse.

On this second day the depth and the menace of the two main German thrusts – towards Stavelot and Trois Ponts in the north and towards Bastogne in the south – became clearer to SHAEF and the two reserve airborne divisions were released to 12th Army Group. They were ordered to move to Bastogne, the best road centre in the Ardennes and a convenient assembly point for their deployment, whenever they were needed by Gen Middleton. Both airborne divisions were near Rheims, short of equipment and with many of their men on leave in Paris. Their XVIII Airborne Corps commander, Maj-Gen Matthew B. Ridgway, was at his rear headquarters in England. The 101st's Commander, Maj-Gen Maxwell D. Taylor, was in Washington and his assistant divisional commander, Brig-Gen Gerald J. Higgins, was in England, lecturing on the earlier airborne operations in Holland.

Maj-Gen James Gavin, normally commanding the 82nd, now acted as corps commander and issued orders that same day, 17 December. By early morning next day both divisions were moving and Gavin himself had reported to First Army headquarters at Spa. Here he was told to send the 82nd to Werbomont to join V Corps and the 101st to Gen Troy Middleton's VIII Corps at Bastogne.

The senior officer left in the 101st was their artillery commander, Brig-Gen Antony C. McAuliffe, and he now took over command of the division. At 4pm on this same day, 18 December, he and his operations staff officer, Lt-Col Harry Kinnard, reached Gen Middleton at his headquarters in a barracks on the outskirts of Bastogne. At the same time Col William L Roberts arrived there with the news that his Combat Command B of the 10th Armored Division was close behind him. This Command, split into three teams, were sent straight on to the east to block the German advance while McAuliffe was told to hold Bastogne itself with his 101st Airborne Division.

Also moving towards Bastogne from the north that evening were the new, self-propelled, long-barrelled 90mm guns of Lt-Col

Clifford D Templeton's 705th Tank Destroyer Battalion. So, by the evening of 18 December, the third day of the battle, the main fighting elements of the Bastogne garrison had reached the town.

As darkness fell and the 101st were driving towards Bastogne, as fast as they could with their headlights on, the 82nd were heading for Werbomont and the task of holding the line of the Salm river against the on-rushing 1st SS Panzer Corps. As the situation worsened, Gen Hodges at First Army began pulling his VII Corps out of the line near Düren, well to the north of the Ardennes, and ordered Gen Lawton J. Collins, 'Lightning Joe', to regroup north of Marche and prepare to counter-attack the Germans from the north with the 2nd and 3rd Armored and the 75th and 84th Infantry Divisions. On the same day Field Marshal Montgomery began to react to the new German threat to both American and British

Left: Belgian refugees moving west over the River Meuse at Dinant on Christmas Day 1944./*US Army*

Above: The bridge over the Meuse at Dinant, completed by US Army engineers on 8 January 1945./*IWM*

Right: Field Marshal Montgomery, newly appointed Colonel Commandant of the Parachute Regiment, wearing their red beret, cap badge and camouflaged smock – in the Ardennes./*IWM*

supply lines and told Gen Brian Horrocks to move XXX Corps with the Guards Armoured, 43rd Wessex, 51st Highland and 53rd Welsh Divisions to Louvain and St Trond, where they would be well placed to attack in flank any German crossing of the Meuse. The British 29th Armoured Brigade was near Brussels, re-equipping with the new Comet tank and they were now ordered to take back their old Shermans and drive at once to guard the Meuse River crossings each side of Dinant.

Lt-Gen John Lee, commanding the US Army Communications Zone and most of the logistic support units behind the battle front, was made responsible for the close defence of the River Meuse, south of Givet and he now ordered four US Engineer regiments and six French infantry battalions to defend the bridges and to join Gen Middleton's VIII Corps.

Next day, 19 December, Ike called a conference at Verdun of the commanders most affected by the German offensive – Bradley 12th Army Group, Patton Third Army, Devers 6th Army Group, and from his own headquarters his Air Deputy, Air Chief Marshal Tedder, and his intelligence chief, Maj-Gen Kenneth Strong. There he arranged for George Patton to drive northwards into the left flank of the German advance with three US divisions on 22 December, the 4th Armored and the 80th and 26th Infantry.

The Allies, and in particular Gen Eisenhower and his staff, had reacted more quickly than Hitler or the German staff had forecast. Within four days of the German attack half a million Allied soldiers were moving towards the Ardennes. While the men of the US V and VIII Corps were fighting desperately to hold or to delay the German armour, the American and British commanders beyond the battle area were concentrating all their efforts and all their resources into plans for massive counter-strokes.

By the time Gen Eisenhower got back to Versailles late on 19 December it was becoming clear to his senior staff officers, Gen Whiteley, Gen Strong and Gen Bedell Smith, that from his 12th Army Group headquarters at Luxembourg Gen Bradley could no longer command effectively the units of the US First and Ninth Armies, fighting north of the German penetrations. They put the problem to Ike, recommending that the only sound solution would be to give command of troops north of the Bulge to Monty, and of those south to Bradley. This might well cause friction, since Monty's abrasive self-assurance had already annoyed many of Bradley's staff and the change could be regarded as a slur on Bradley's capability, yet Eisenhower hardly hesitated. Taking a map, he drew a line from Givet on the Meuse to Prüm in the Siegfried Line. Both army group commanders were told of Ike's decision that same night and formal orders were issued next morning. Monty at once sent off his liaison officers to visit every American headquarters, now coming under his command, and set off himself to visit Gen Simpson at the US Ninth Army and Gen Hodges at the US First Army – wearing the airborne, camouflaged smock and red beret of the Parachute Regiment, of which he had just been made Colonel Commandant.

9 The 1st SS Panzer Division Thrust to the West

Obersturmbannführer Jochen Peiper's battlegroup of tanks, infantry and egineers reached Stavelot on the evening of 17 December after a long and action-packed day. The rest of the 1st SS Panzer Division were miles behind, held up by colossal traffic jams east of Bullingen, and the 3rd Parachute Division were in action at Waimes and Faymonville eight miles behind him. The 12th SS Panzer Division should by now have come up on his right, driving through Malmedy but they had been unable to break the stubborn defences of the US 99th and 2nd Infantry Divisions round Krinkelt, Rocherath and Butgenbach and were still heavily engaged 14 miles to the east. Looking down at Stavelot from the hill east of the Amblève River bridge, Peiper could see that the town was jammed with American trucks. These were mostly from a transport company moving north to Francorchamps, where attempts were being made to shift to the west a First Army fuel dump of 2½ million gallons. The only fighting troops in Stavelot were a squad of the US 291st Engineer

Battalion, who had set up a road block with mines and a bazooka on the south side of the bridge. The bazooka man scored a hit on the leading tank and Peiper gave orders for a night halt.

During the night Maj Paul Solis's company of the 526th Armored Infantry in half-tracks with some three-inch anti-tank guns reached Stavelot, but Peiper's infantry and tanks drove them out of the town to the north in a dawn attack next day, 18 December.

The attack was led by Lt Kremser's 1st Panzer Company and Maj Diefenthal's 3rd Panzer Grenadier Battalion. A shell killed Kremser, Lt Hennecke took his place, an American six-pounder gun knocked out a Panther tank, the American demolition charges on the bridge failed to detonate and by 10am Peiper's men were fighting hard in Stavelot itself. Maj Solis finally pulled his men back, north of the town towards Francorchamps and the fuel dump. Here, helped by a Belgian officer, he built a massive barricade of full petrol cans across the road where it ran through a wood,

Above left: Bernard Arnest's drawing of Stavelot, scene of fierce fighting between the 1st SS Panzer Division, men of the US 291st Engineers, the 56th Armored Infantry Battalion and the 30th Division./*US Army*

Left: Another drawing by Standley of Stavelot. This view is from north of the Ambleve river and was drawn from the command post of the 117th Infantry. Peiper's original attack had rolled down the road from the hill across the valley./*US Army*

Above: Men of the 30th Division clearing the burned out jerricans from Paul Solis's flaming road block on the road to Francorchamps./*IWM*

Right: Another of Bernard Arnest's drawings. It shows the key bridge over the Salm river at Trois Ponts, blown in the nick of time by men of the 51st Engineers./*US Army*

Left: A Piper Cub or L-19 aircraft, flown by Maj Jack Blohm, fitted with skis for the Ardennes conditions./*US Army*

Right: Infantry of the 117th Regiment. /*US Army*

Below right: The bridge at Malmedy on 22 December, firmly held by the 117th Infantry, but prepared for demolition – white tapes mark the safe way over./*US Army*

but Peiper's tanks, led by Hennecke had already turned westwards and were racing on towards the next bridge over the River Salm at Trois Ponts.

Paul Solis fired his barricade, but the German tanks had not followed him up the Francorchamps road. Later that morning the 117th Infantry of the 30th Division reached the dump on their way to re-take Stavelot and their commanding officer ordered the burning to stop.

Trois Ponts was only four miles further on. Here there were three bridges, two over the Salm and one over the Amblève. Only the day before, at midnight on 17 December, Maj Robert Yates's Company C, 51st Engineers, had reached Trois Ponts, rushed there from their job of operating sawmills in the forests of the Ardennes. Maj Robert Yates had 140 men, 10 machine guns and eight bazookas and at once set up road blocks covering the bridge over the Amblève and the road from Stavelot. While his men began preparing the main road bridge for demolition, he put a squad forward near the railway bridge over the main road. Soon afterwards a single six-pounder anti-tank gun and crew, looking for their company of the 526th Armored Infantry in Stavelot, came driving by and Yates commandeered them, placing the gun under the railway bridge, facing east.

At 11.45am 19 German tanks appeared and opened fire on the men working at the river bridge. As the leading tank neared the railway bridge, the American six-pounder scored a first-time hit and the tank stopped. For 15 minutes the German tank gunners searched for the single, small American gun and finally destroyed it with a direct hit, killing all four crewmen – McCollum, Hollen-beck, Buchanan and Higgins – but just as the German tanks began to roll forward, two explosions shook the town and showered the river road with debris. The American engineers had blown both bridges over the Amblève and the Salm.

Cursing his luck, Peiper now turned his troops northwards, up the road towards La Gleize and Stoumont, the only route still open to him. A narrow road led off to the left to Cheneux and a bridge over the Salm and this was now the route which he chose for his continuing drive to the west. His leading tanks found the bridge intact and drove on towards Werbomont, but now the skies had cleared and for the first time Piper Cubs of the 109th Tactical Reconnaissance Squadron spotted his column, and four Thunderbolts of the 365th Fighter Group dived to the attack. Two tanks and seven half-tracks were knocked out, but a much

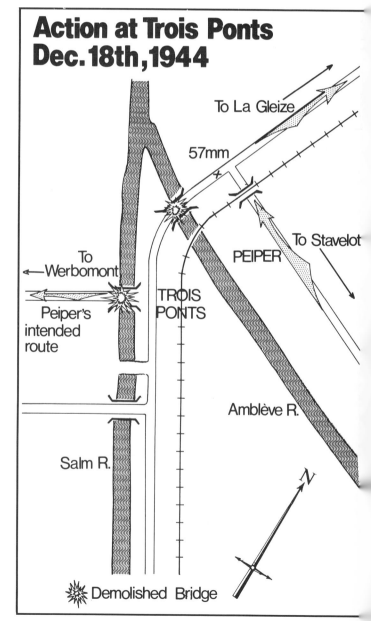

Action at Trois Ponts Dec. 18th, 1944

To La Gleize

57mm

To Werbomont ←

Peiper's intended route

TROIS PONTS

PEIPER

To Stavelot

Salm R.

Amblève R.

N

※ Demolished Bridge

greater frustration for Jochen Peiper was the sound of another bridge blowing up in front of his leading tanks. This was the bridge over the River Lienne near Chevron, where yet another squad of Americans from the 291st Engineer Battalion had got there just in time to prevent Peiper's tanks reaching Werbomont and a clear run to the Meuse.

One detachment of half-tracks and assault guns found another bridge further north, but as they crossed it and turned south-west towards Werbomont, they ran into an ambush laid by Maj Hal McCown's 2nd Battalion 119th Infantry, who destroyed all the German vehicles. This was a unit of the US 30th Infantry Division

now moving rapidly south to block the advance north-west of Peiper's column. By this time too, the US 82nd Airborne Division were closing in on Peiper from the west, although he was not yet aware of the trap into which he was heading. So, on the evening of 18 December, Peiper's battlegroup of the 1st SS Panzer Division was approaching Stoumont, and he had realised that his only way to the west was through this village. Allied planes had located his force and both V Corps and First Army could now complete the blocking of his routes forwards. The 117th Infantry from the 30th Division reached Malmedy and Stavelot early on 18 December and the 1st Battalion attacked and re-captured Stavelot, driving

Above: Two men of the 30th Division engage a low-flying German fighter aircraft at Francorchamps on 27 December./*US Army*

Right: US troops dig in under fire. One of them lies dead in the foreground./*IWM*

out of it the small garrison left there by Peiper, blowing the Amblève River bridge and cutting his supply line from the rest of the 1st SS Panzer Division. The 119th Infantry reached Stoumont late on 18 December, sending the 2nd Battalion round to block the road westwards through Werbomont; putting the 3rd into Stoumont itself and positioning the 1st in reserve on the high ground north of the town.

The Sixth SS Panzer Army's drive to the west was slowing down. Its spear-point, Peiper's battlegroup, had been blocked at Trois Ponts and Cheneux and looked like having a stiff fight, if they were to break through the 119th Infantry in Stoumont. They were already cut off from fuel and ammunition supplies by the 117th Infantry at Stavelot. The German 3rd Parachute Division, who were supposed to be close behind Peiper, were heavily engaged at Waimes and Faymonville, holding the northern flank of the German corridor. The 12th SS Panzer Division were still fighting fiercely to break through the US 99th, 2nd and 1st Divisions on the Butgen-bach–Malmedy road and instead of being up on Peiper's right, galloping for the Meuse, they were taking heavy casualties 20 miles behind him. Worse still, the Sixth SS Panzer Army's second wave, the 9th SS Panzer and 2nd SS Panzer Divisions were held up back at the Siegfried Line by the traffic chaos in the narrow corridor ahead of them.

Early in the morning of 19 December Peiper launched an attack on Stoumont. With him in La Gleize he had a mixed battalion of Mark IV and Mark V Panthers from the 1st SS Panzer Regiment, some Mark VI Tigers, a battalion from the 2nd SS Panzer Grena-diers, a flak unit, a battery of tracked 105mm guns and a company om the 3rd Parachute Division, riding on his tanks. In the town as the US 3rd Battalion, 119th Infantry with the guns of the 23rd Tank Destroyer Battalion but without artillery support. The German infantry and tanks fought their way into the town and in wo hours of fierce fighting at close quarters, destroyed two out of three American infantry companies.

The 1st Battalion 119th Infantry, in reserve, north of the town, withdrew steadily and in good order through Targnon to Stoumont station, helped by 10 tanks from the 743rd Tank Battalion, and knocking out several German tanks as they followed up. The 197th Field Artillery now came into action behind them and as the German armour moved out of Targnon it was met by an intense concentration of shell-fire and disappeared back into the village. Peiper, in fact, had no wish to drive on northwards and would have turned west again at Targnon, if his fuel stocks had allowed it. His tanks were running dry, however, and he now concentrated his battle-group in Stoumont, La Gleize and Cheneux.

Ten more tanks arrived to reinforce the American 119th, led by Capt James Berry of the 740th Tank Battalion. He and his men, many of them Ordnance Corps Mechanics, had drawn them from the First Army repair shops that morning. Some of the Shermans had British radios, which the American crews could not operate; some of them were DD or duplex-drive, swimming tanks, used in the D-Day invasion; and a 90mm self-propelled anti-tank gun was thrown in for good measure.

The same day, 19 December, the 82nd Airborne Division reached Werbomont and began pushing eastwards to find the enemy. The 504th Parachute Infantry reached Rahier on the road to La Gleize; the 505th pushed out to Basse-Bodeux towards Trois Ponts and the 325th Glider Infantry were rushed to Hotton some miles away to the south-west on rumours of German armour thrusting westwards from Bastogne.

Moving in from the north was the US 3rd Armored Division, with Combat Command B advancing to the support of the 117th Infantry in Stavelot and the 119th in Stoumont, while the rest of the division were directed to the west of the 82nd Airborne to hold the German columns driving for the Meuse from Houffalize and Bastogne.

On 20 December all these American forces, converging on the German spearhead in Stoumont and La Gleize, went over to the attack. The 1st Battalion 119th Infantry with the tanks of the 740th struck through Targnon. Company C with Lt Powers and five

Left: A wounded man, brought in on a sledge, is transferred to a stretcher jeep by medical orderlies of the 119th Infantry in Stoumont. /*US Army*

Below: A Mark VI Tiger II which ran out of fuel on the Stavelot road. /*IWM*

Shermans led off through the fog and at once met a Panther at close range. Powers fired, hit the Panther's gun mantlet and killed the German's gunner. Driving on, he saw a Tiger, fired at it twice and each time the shell bounced off. Powers' gun then jammed and he radioed for help as the Tiger fired its 88mm gun and luckily missed Powers' Sherman. By now the lone tank destroyer had come up and with one shot from its 90mm gun turned the Tiger into a smoking wreck.

A second Panther appeared out of the fog and Powers fired again, his shell bouncing off the road, penetrating the floor of the German tank, setting it on fire. All this encouraged Company C and by nightfall they were in the big sanatorium on the outskirts of Stoumont. Then in the night the Germans stormed back and with their tanks firing into the building from 20 yards away, a ferocious struggle raged through every floor, while 200 old people and invalids crouched in the cellars. By morning the Germans had re-captured the sanatorium, except for a small annex, in which Sgt William Widener and 11 men held out all next day.

Task Force Jordan from the 3rd Armored Division tried to enter Stoumont from the north down the Spa road, but were driven back with the loss of two tanks by German Panthers, cunningly sited in

Left: A bazooka team of Company C, 325th Glider Infantry near Hotton./*US Army*

Below: Men of the 117th Infantry searching a house in the fight to recapture Stavelot on 20 December./*US Army*

Right: Men from the US 30th Division bring in a wounded German. /*US Army*

Below right: Men of the 2nd Bn 504th Parachute Infantry on the march to Cheneux./*US Army*

the houses. On the far side of La Gleize, however, another part of Combat Command B, Task Force Lovelady, succeeded in cutting the road between La Gleize and Trois Ponts and destroying a German transport column, trying to reach Peiper with supplies.

Col Reuben Tucker's 504th Parachute Infantry came under heavy fire, as they neared Cheneux that afternoon and waited until it was dark. Then the 1st Battalion attacked over 400 yards of open ground and took terrible losses from the intense fire of mortars and machine guns of the 2nd SS Panzer Grenadiers in the village.

On their third attempt the parachute troops got a foothold in the outlying houses and there they waited all next day. In the evening another company reached them and fighting went on all night, mostly with bayonet, knife and grenade. On 22 December Julian Cook's 3rd Battalion made a six-hour march right round Cheneux to attack from the north, and by the evening the battle was over. The 504th had lost 225 men dead and wounded, but very few of the SS Panzer Grenadiers survived and 14 20mm flak wagons and a battery of 105mm howitzers fell into American hands.

While the fight for Cheneux was going on, all three battalions of the 119th Infantry were attacking Stoumont again from the west, north and east, but in each case without success, except that the Americans finally took back the Stoumont Sanatorium on the night of 21 December, getting four Shermans right up to the building. A snowstorm next morning prevented much action, but at noon the three American battalions moved in once more. This time they met no fire and found only German wounded and dead and some American prisoners in the town. Peiper had withdrawn all his movable vehicles and men to La Gleize. Priess, his corps com-

mander, now asked Sixth Army if Peiper could be allowed to break back to the east to rejoin the rest of the 1st SS Panzer Division south of Stavelot. Permission was refused and Peiper continued to hold out in La Gleize against American attacks through 23 December.

This was the day the weather cleared and the Allied air forces swarmed over the battle area with devastating effect on the German columns. Six aircraft of the 329th Bombardment Group were tasked to bomb the German Seventh Army railhead at Zulpich and thought they had struck Lammersum, six miles northeast of Zulpich. In fact their bombs fell on Malmedy, 39 miles to the west, setting the town on fire and killing 37 men of the American 120th Infantry and many civilians. Protests flew up the chain of command, but the unfortunate town was bombed twice more, on Christmas Eve and Christmas Day, by what the soldiers of the 120th called the American Luftwaffe. Then on the night of 23 December Wilhelm Mohnke, Peiper's divisional commander, got through to him on the radio, ordering him to break out to the east. Without petrol and burdened with casualties he could only move on foot and at 1am he set out with 800 men in single file, through the woods along the Amblève River. Passing north of Trois Ponts and crossing the Salm river, he rejoined his division on Christmas morning.

When the 30th Division troops entered La Gleize on the morning of Christmas Eve, they found some 170 Americans, most of them captured five days before in Stoumont, and 300 German wounded. 28 German tanks, 25 self-propelled guns and 70 half-tracks left in the town showed that, taking into account other losses along the road to La Gleize, the 1st SS Panzer Division had lost almost all its armoured strength.

It took two more days of sharp fighting to clear the woods round La Gleize and Stoumont of the remnants of Peiper's battlegroup. S/Sgt Paul Bolden and T/Sgt Russell Snoad attacked a house full of Germans, Bolden running in under cover of Snoads' rifle fire, to toss two grenades in through the door. Following the bursts, Bolden jumped inside, killing 20 men with his Thompson gun, but as he dodged outside again, he was wounded and Snoad killed by a burst of fire from the house. Dashing back in again Bolden killed or wounded all the remaining 15 Germans in the house.

While the leading battlegroup of the 1st SS Panzer Division, led by Jochen Peiper, were driving west to their final destruction in

La Gleize, the rest of the division were being assembled south of Stavelot by their commander, Wilhelm Mohnke. Although most of his tank strength was gone, he still had his reconnaissance battalion, a mixed unit of tanks, armoured cars and infantry in half-tracks, the best part of the 22nd Panzer Grenadier Regiment, and his artillery and assault guns. With these troops he struck at the Salm river line, meeting the 505th Parachute Infantry at Trois Ponts and La Neuville, who were able to prevent any Germans crossing the Salm river. Another detachment tried and failed to cross the Amblève and to reach Peiper. On 26 December the remnants of the division were ordered south to join the Fifth Panzer Army's attacks on Bastogne and the remaining tanks of the division were knocked out in the US Third Army's assault from the south early in the new year.

To speed the Sixth SS Panzer Army and its spearhead, the 1st SS Panzer Division, on their way to the Meuse and thence onwards to Brussels and Antwerp, four special operations were planned and mounted. The first, with code-name Hohes Venn, was a parachute

attack by an improvised battalion of 1,000 men, led by Col Friedrich Baron von der Heydte, who were to drop north of Malmedy to prevent enemy reinforcements moving south and to hold open roads to the north-west for the German armour. Von der Heydte was commanding the parachute school in Aalten and only received these orders on 8 December. Some 112 Ju52 transport aircraft were allotted to him, but many of the pilots had never dropped parachute troops. On 11 December his scratch force moved to Sennelager, near the take-off airfields of Paderborn and Lippspringe. On the 12th Von der Heydte received final orders from Sepp Dietrich, who appeared to be drunk and on the subject of parachute troops was both contemptuous and insulting. Troops were supposed to move to their airfields on the 15th, but no transport arrived. Finally they got into the air 24 hours late and dropped at dawn on 17 December. One rifle company landed near Bonn, 50 miles east of the drop zone, most of the signal platoon came down near Monschau and the rest were scattered over a wide area. About 300 finally reached the rendezvous on the Eupen road near Mount Rigi and after some ineffectual patrolling, von der Heydte gave orders for the group to disperse and make their own way back to the German

Left: A patrol of the 3rd Battalion 18th Infantry searching the woods near Eupen for von der Heydte's parachute troops./*US Army*

Below: Two soldiers, Thomas Richardson and George Leach find a German parachute in these same woods – and the rumours start!/*IWM*

Right: A .50cal machine gun of the 120th Infantry covering the road into Malmedy on 22 December./*US Army*

Below right: Assault gun of Panzer Brigade 150, painted with the white star of Allied forces and knocked out in the attack on Malmedy. Two American engineers are checking it for booby-traps./*US Army*

lines. He himself walked into Monschau on 21 December to find the town still safely in American hands and himself a prisoner of war.

There were three ground operations. Raiding parties in American uniforms and riding in captured American tanks and jeeps were to dash ahead of the German armour, once the American defences were breached, to seize intact the Meuse bridges. Following up to reinforce these bridge assault parties was the 150th Panzer Brigade (Brandenburger), equivalent to a strong battalion and also equipped with a few American Shermans. Once the Meuse bridges were secure, specially trained English-speaking 'Kommandos', each of four German volunteers in American uniforms and in an American jeep, were to drive into the Allied rear areas to create as much confusion as they could by sabotage of communications.

In a personal interview Adolf Hitler gave these ground tasks to Obersturmbannführer Otto Skorzeny, together with the responsibility for raising and training Panzer Brigade 150. Skorzeny had already made his name by taking part in the rescue of Mussolini on 12 September 1943, the day after the Italian capitulation. Ten gliders, full of men of Oberleutnant Freiherr von Berlepsch's company from the Maj Mors' Parachute Training Battalion, briefed personally by Gen Student, landed on the Gran Sasso mountain, while the rest of the battalion secured the valley road and railway below. Skorzeny flew in a glider as an SS representative and flew out with Mussolini in a Fieseler Storch light aircraft to Rome. Thence he took Mussolini in a Heinkel He111 to the Führer's headquarters in Rastenburg, where he claimed to have planned and led the whole coup de main himself – much to the annoyance of Gen Student and his parachute troops. Later on he had captured the Citadel in Budapest, seat of the Hungarian Government in another coup de main, kidnapping the son of Admiral Horthy, the Regent of Hungary.

Since no breakthrough was achieved by the 1st SS Panzer Corps, Skorzeny's Panzer Brigade 150 were never able to start for the

Meuse bridges. On 21 December they were used in a normal ground role to attack Malmedy in an effort to break loose the American hold on the Northern shoulder or 'door-post' of the Bulge, but were beaten back with heavy losses by the US 30th Division. Soon afterwards they were disbanded and sent as reinforcements to other SS divisions and Skorzeny returned to Germany.

Several of his 'Kommandos' did succeed, however, in reaching the American rear areas. One jeep-load was captured by British troops at Dinant and another by American Military police near Liège. News of these parties and of the abortive parachute drop north of Malmedy spread rapidly from the front lines back to Paris and had a significant effect in spreading confusion and alarm. American and British officers were stopped and arrested on suspicion, if they could not answer weirdly topical questions on American sporting and entertainment stars, and attempts were made to restrict Gen Eisenhower's movements, because of rumours of a plot to assassinate him. Eighteen of Skorzeny's men, mostly captured at Dinant, near Malmedy and elsewhere and all caught in United States Army uniforms were court-martialled and shot at Henri-Chappelle or Huy. Only three teams got back to the German lines.

Above left: SS soldier in American uniform, killed near Hotton on 26 December./*US Army*

Left: US Military police check the credentials of Belgian civilians./*IWM*

Above: US Military police from the 84th Infantry Division at a checkpoint near Marche./*US Army*

Right: Pvt Casper checks a civilian in the 9th Armored Division sector near Ermsdorf on 26 December, while Pvt Beckemeyer mans the .50cal machine gun./*US Army*

Right: Cpl Harris in the 7th Armored Division arriving at St Vith is checked by Pvt Dopp./*US Army*

Centre right: One of Skorzeny's men captured by the 30th Division near Malmedy./*IWM*

Bottom right: Officer Cadet Gunther Billing, Cpl Wilhelm Schmidt and Sgt Manfred Pernass are shot, after court martial. They were one of Skorzeny's groups, wearing American uniforms, carrying American weapons and driving in a jeep, when captured. /*IWM*

10 The Battle for St Vith

Left: Aerial view of St Vith after the battle.
/*US Army*

The town of St Vith at the junction of six main roads is the centre of road communications in the northern part of the Ardennes. The main routes to the west chosen by the German Army Group B for Sepp Dietrich's Sixth SS Panzer Army ran north of the town and those for von Manteuffel's Fifth Panzer Army to the south of it, but the German command could not afford to by-pass the town completely, as its road net was essential for the secure movement of supplies and the ability to switch reserves laterally, as the situation demanded. On 16 December St Vith lay 12 miles behind the American front lines. In the town were the headquarters of the US 106th Infantry Division and a number of the divisional maintenance and supply units. As the German LXVI Corps pressed forward round the north and south flanks of the US 106th Division on the morning of 16 December and the 1st SS Panzer Division burst through the Losheim Gap, Gen Middleton and VIII Corps headquarters in Bastogne and Gen Jones in his 106th Division command post in St Vith soon realised the size of the German threat. On Gen Middleton's order Brig-Gen Hoge's Combat Command B of the 9th Armored Division reached St Vith late on that same day and at 5.30pm the order to move to St Vith from Gen Gerow's V Corps reached Brig-Gen Robert Hasbrouck's 7th Armored Division in their reserve billets north of Aachen. Two hours later he and his advance parties were on their way to Bastogne, where Troy Middleton told Hasbrouck to move two combat commands to St Vith as fast as possible. At 4.30am next day, 17 December, the division started south. Combat Command B was at

Vielsalm by 11am, but it took them five hours to cover the 14 miles from Vielsalm to St Vith along roads, choked with American traffic, fleeing to the west. Gen Jones in St Vith now needed tanks urgently. His two forward regiments were trapped on the Schnee Eifel and German troops were in Setz only four miles east of St Vith. An engineer regiment, the 168th, was dug in on the edge of the pine forest two miles from the town, Combat Command B of the 9th Armored and the 424th Infantry were fighting to hold the German 62nd Volksgrenadier Division near Steinebrück in the south-east and a troop of light tanks from the 89th Cavalry Squadron were holding Wallerode to the north-east. Yet the 7th Armored Division's leading unit, Brig-Gen Bruce Clarke's Combat Com-B, could hardly move on the road in from the west. Supply vehicles, officers in jeeps, artillery towing vehicles without their guns and trucks of all sorts were driving westwards, two and three abreast, in considerable disorder. It took determined action by Gen Has-

Below left: Brig-Gen William Hoge, who led Combat Command B of the 9th Armored Division in the struggle for St Vith./*US Army*

Below: Brig-Gen Robert Hasbrouck, who commanded the 7th Armored Division and later the whole garrison of St Vith. He is seen here in April 1945, after his promotion to Maj-Gen, talking to some of his officers./*US Army*

Right: Harrison Standley's picture of St Vith./*US Army*

brouck himself and the threat of ramming by the oncoming tanks to clear a road to St Vith for these vital reinforcements. Behind them the rest of the 7th Armored Division were following on towards St Vith, just missing Jochen Peiper's tanks south of Stavelot as they crossed his road westwards.

By nightfall on 17 December, the second day of the battle, US units had formed a horse-shoe defence round St Vith. Recht, five miles to the north-west, was held by the US 17th Tank Battalion and in the village was the command post of Combat Command R, 7th Armored. With them were a few disorganised remnants of the 14th Cavalry, who had fallen back before the German onrush through the Losheim Gap. From Hünningen to the St Vith–Schönberg road the line was held by the 87th Cavalry Squadron, the 168th Engineers and Combat Command B, 7th Armored. From there down through Lammersweiler to Burg Reuland were Combat Command B, 9th Armored and the 424th Infantry, all that was left of the 106th Division. Six miles away to their west and behind them at Beho was Combat Command A, 7th Armored, and in action west of St Vith were the 105mm guns of the 275th and 16th Armored Field Artillery.

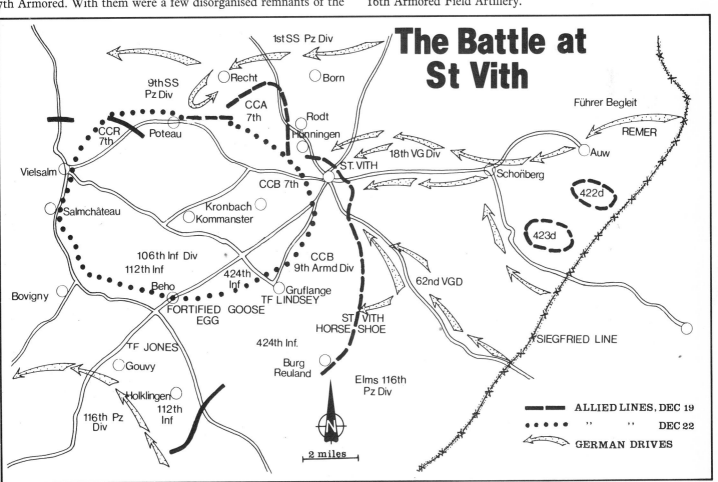

The Battle at St Vith

ALLIED LINES, DEC 19
" " DEC 22
GERMAN DRIVES

2 miles

To the south of this defensive line little was left of the US 28th Division and the German LVIII Panzer Corps were driving westwards. One regiment of the 28th Division, Col Austin Nelson's 112th Infantry were retreating in good order to the north-west and on the next day joined the defence of St Vith, facing south, on the right flank of the 424th near Burg Reuland.

Luckily for the Americans forming this hasty defence, Gen Lucht's LXVI Corps spent most of the 17th unscrambling their own traffic jams, made worse by the inability of his SS neighbours in Gen Priess's SS Panzer Corps to clear more than one road forward and their tendency to encroach on the roads further south, allotted to Lucht's divisions.

At 2am on 18 December, the third day of the battle, the American tank company in Recht, north of St Vith, was attacked by a strong force of SS Panzer Grenadiers and assault guns and after 45 minutes of brisk shooting, Combat Command R, 7th Armored withdrew to Poteau, two miles west. This was a second battle-group of the 1st SS Panzer Division, consisting of the 2nd SS Panzer Grenadier Regiment and a battalion of assault guns and they were miles behind Peiper and his 1st SS Panzer Regiment whom they were supposed to be supporting. Two hours later they attacked again at Poteau, driving the American tanks and armoured cars out of the village and capturing eight eight-inch howitzers abandoned there by the US 740th Field Artillery Battalion. The emnants of Combat Command R and the 14th Cavalry joined a scratch force of US tanks, infantry and engineers a few miles to the west, calling themselves Task Force Navaho, and there they took up defensive positions once more, looking rather desperately up the road from Poteau and expecting a third attack at any moment. But the German battlegroup were not interested in them and swung northwards to reach Peiper's force at La Gleize, spending the next few days in vain attempts to cross the Amblève and Salm rivers, beaten back each time by the US 30th Infantry and 82nd Airborne Divisions.

That same morning, while the SS Panzer Grenadiers were driving round the north of St Vith, another attack by the 18th Volksgrenadiers came in at Hünningen. Only two cavalry troops and some anti-aircraft machine guns were defending the village, but two companies of Shermans, under Maj Leonard Engemann from the 14th Tank Battalion, supported by a company of the 811th Tank Destroyer Battalion, circled round the German attack and drove them back with heavy losses. East of St Vith the 38th and 23rd Armored Infantry Battalions broke up two German attacks, greatly helped by the accurate fire of the 275th Armored Artillery, whose forward observers always seemed to be in the right place at the right time and whose guns played a major part in stopping a succession of German attacks all round St Vith.

Down in the south-east corner of the St Vith defences the 62nd Volksgrenadiers finally forced back the US 9th Armored Division

Left: A 105mm battery in position west of St Vith, ready to answer calls for fire./*US Army*

Below left: An 8in howitzer on the move up to support the 7th Armored Armored Division./*US Army*

Below: Men of the 23rd Armored Infantry go to ground near St Vith, as fire is opened./*US Army*

Bottom: Harrison Standley's picture of Poteau, where the US 40th Tank Battalion and 48th Armored Infantry held off the second battle group of the 1st SS Panzer Division and later units of the 9th SS Panzer Division./*US Army*

Above: Company C of the 48th Armored Infantry near St Vith./*US Army*

Left: Gen Bittrich, commanding the II SS Panzer Corps./*Bundesarchiv*

Bottom left: Col Otto Remer, wearing his Knight's Cross and two tank crewmen. /*Bundesarchiv*

Above right: Harrison Standley's drawing of Echelrath, where Company B of the 27th Armored Infantry beat off the 190th Grenadier Regiment on 19 December./*US Army*

Right: A Sherman tank crew refuelling and rearming./*US Army*

and the 424th Infantry to within three miles of St Vith, while seven miles away to the south-west at Gouvy a scratch force based on the 440th Anti-Aircraft Battalion under Lt-Col Jones fought off a probing German column from the 116th Panzer Division, now chasing hard for Houffalize. In the afternoon of this day, 18 December, Combat Command A, 7th Armored, who were still in reserve, were launched in an attack to regain Poteau and by nightfall the 48th Armored Infantry and the 40th Tanks were firmly established there. So by the evening of the third day German armour had reached Trois Ponts, some 10 miles north-west of St Vith and were past Gouvy 10 miles to the south-west. The front of this St Vith salient was still holding and continued to hold through the next day, 19 December, as German probing attacks came in all round the perimeter.

In the north at Poteau the 9th SS Panzer Division appeared for the first time. This was part of Gen Bittrich's follow-up II Panzer Corps of the Sixth SS Panzer Army and their attempt to enter Poteau was defeated without much difficulty. At the command post of the 18th Volksgrenadier Division two great men arrived to see what was happening, Field Marshal Model, commanding Army Group B and Gen von Manteuffel from the Fifth Panzer Army. There they met Gen Lucht, LXVI Corps, and Gen Hoffman-Schönborn of the 18th Division and made it clear that Lucht was to take St Vith at all costs and as soon as possible. To

help the 18th and 62nd Volksgrenadier Divisions in this task, they gave Lucht the Führer Begleit Brigade, led by Col Otto Remer and made up of three panzer grenadier battalions, a battalion of Mark IV tanks, another of assault guns, an artillery battalion and eight flak batteries. Formed originally as an escort for Hitler, they were at full strength and in a high state of training. Remer had made his name in the abortive putsch of July 1944, when his prompt action in Berlin had contributed largely to the failure of the plot. On their way forward to join the LXVI Corps, they had rolled through the US 422nd Infantry on the Schnee Eifel, giving them the final blow which led to the surrender of both the 422nd and 423rd Infantry.

Next day the Germans continued their probing attacks towards St Vith, but without launching the major assault, ordered by Model and Manteuffel. In the 18th Volksgrenadiers traffic chaos prevented any sensible movement, except for an attack from Wallerode by the 295th Grenadier Regiment, which withered away under intense American artillery fire. The divisional commander, Gen Hoffman-Schönborn, who had come forward to cheer them on, was badly wounded in this bombardment. In the south-east the 62nd Volksgrenadiers were equally unsuccessful, as their 190th Grenadiers made the mistake of advancing in close formation against the US 27th Armored Infantry in Echelrath and were mown down in swathes.

Left: Aerial view of part of the battle west of St Vith. Seven or eight knocked out armoured vehicles are visible, half covered by subsequent snowfalls./*US Army*

Above: Another Standley drawing. This shows the railway at Crombach, south west of St Vith, where Combat Command B, 7th Armored and the guns of the 434th Field Artillery just managed to hold off the 190th Grenadiers on 23 December, as the German infantry and tanks advanced along the railway./*US Army*

This was also the day when Gen Eisenhower split the command, placing the US First and Ninth Armies in the north of the Ardennes under Field Marshal Montgomery's 21st Army Group and everything south of the line Givet on the Meuse to Prüm under Gen Hodge's 12th Army Group. Gen Middleton's VIII Corps, fighting to hold the armoured spearheads of the Fifth Panzer Army, as they drove round the north of Bastogne, now came under Gen Patton's Third Army, while Gen Gerow's V Corps, holding the northern shoulder round Elsenborn, and Gen Ridgway's XVIII Airborne Corps, moving up on Gerow's right flank, came under Gen Hodge's First Army and Monty's 21st Army Group.

At Monty's request, Maj-Gen J. Lawton Collins, whom he considered the best American corps commander, with his VII Corps headquarters, was now added to First Army and the 2nd and 3rd Armored Divisions and 75th and 84th Infantry Divisions were placed in his corps. The whole corps began moving south to cover the vulnerable right flank of First Army and to deal with the German armour, still driving for the Meuse.

On 21 December Gen Lucht's LXVI Corps finally moved forward in a coordinated attack to take St Vith. The Führer Begleit Brigade crashed their way round the north of the town and got as far as the gun lines of the US 275th Armored Field Artillery, before they were stopped by the point-blank fire of the self-propelled 105s. In a series of attacks with heavy artillery support the 18th and 62nd Volksgrenadier Divisions slowly pushed back the 7th Armored Division, 38th and 23rd Armored Infantry and the remnants of the 424th. By nightfall the German infantry has got into the town, most of the forward companies of the American infantry were overrun and a new American defence line was set up with great difficulty west of St Vith. There they held out against renewed attacks by the Führer Begleit Brigade from Roth in the north and the 62nd Volksgrenadiers in the south, helped considerably by a colossal German traffic jam in St Vith, where units of both the 18th and 62nd Volksgrenadier Divisions and of the Sixth Panzer Army were trying to get forward through the narrow streets of the town, their normal complement of motor vehicles and horses swollen by captured American jeeps and trucks. Even Field Marshal Model's car could not get through and he had to get out and walk into the town.

By the morning of 22 December things were desperate in the defensive circle west of St Vith. The men of the two Combat Command Bs of 7th and 9th Armored Divisions had lost half their tanks and were very tired. The armoured infantry battalions had suffered heavy casualties and the 424th Infantry were equally battered. Food, fuel and ammunition were more and more difficult to bring forward and the German attacks were intensifying. Gen Robert Hasbrouck from his 7th Armored Division headquarters in Vielsalm sent an urgent message to his new Corps Commander, Gen Matthew Ridgway, advising withdrawal behind the Salm river. A British liaison officer and a British Phantom Signal Regiment radio link reached Vielsalm and reported directly to Field Marshal Montgomery on the situation west of St Vith. By the middle of the afternoon the order to withdraw through Vielsalm reached Hasbrouck from Ridgway with an additional message from Monty, 'they can come back with all honour. . .'

Hasbrouck and his chief staff officer, Col Ryan, sat down at once to plan the most difficult of all operations – a withdrawal, in close contact with a superior enemy. Through 23 December his units fell back in good order, covered by rearguards of tanks, infantry and guns, while the Germans followed them up as best they could. By dark they were all over the Vielsalm bridge and

west of the Salm river, now firmly held by the 82nd Airborne Division. Only in the south was there a disaster, where Task Force Jones, consisting of tanks, tank destroyers, engineers and infantry only got the order to withdraw after a three-hour delay and on reaching the bridge at Salmchateau, found it blown. At the same time they were attacked by the Führer Begleit Brigade, now driving south-west to join the LVIII Corps, and although a few tanks and guns broke away to the west and reached the 82nd Division line, most of the Task Force was destroyed.

The losses in the 106th Infantry Division, the 14th Cavalry Group, the 7th Armored and the 9th Armored Divisions had been very heavy, but they had held up the advance of the German LXVI Corps for a week, they had prevented any expansion of the gap created by Peiper's battlegroup and they had severely damaged the German 18th and 62nd Divisions.

Below: A drawing by Standley of Salmchateau, facing north west and towards the positions held by the 82nd Airborne Division./*US War Dept*

Bottom: A 3in anti-tank gun, covering a road out of Vielsalm./*US Army*

Right: A 7th Armored Division .50 calibre machine gun in position near Vielsalm./*US Army*

Below right: Three German assault guns and a Volkswagen, knocked out on a road near St Vith./*US Army*

Left: Five Shermans knocked out in the battle for St Vith./*IWM*

Right: One hundred B-26 light bombers from the US 9th Air Force bombing St Vith on Christmas Day – after its capture by the Germans./*US Air Force*

Below: Gen Quesada, 9th Air Force, inspects the damage in St Vith in January 1945, after the recapture of the town by the 7th Armored Division./*US Air Force*

11 The Battle for Bastogne

While the Americans fought to hold St Vith in the north of the Ardennes, the struggle was beginning further south for the equally important road centre at Bastogne. On 16 and 17 December five German divisions had torn a great hole in the American lines, destroying the US 110th Infantry and driving back the two other regiments of the 28th Division to north and south. The only reserves now left to Gen Middleton, commanding the US VIII Corps in Bastogne, were two engineer regiments and Combat Command Reserve of the 9th Armored Division and these small forces he now sent out to do what they could to delay the advancing German armour. On 18 December the 25th and 158th Engineer Battalions were in position at Foy, Bizory, Neffe and Marvie on the roads into Bastogne from the north-east, east and south-east and the armour had set up two forward road blocks at Lallange and Allerborn. Task Force Rose at Lallange, a company of tanks, another of infantry and a platoon of sappers, were in action early on the 18th with the armoured cars, half-tracks and tanks of the 2nd Panzer Reconnaissance Battalion and a little later were surrounded by the Mark IV and Mark V Panther tanks of the 3rd Panzer Regiment. In the intense fire-fight, which followed, the Americans suffered heavy losses and when the survivors tried to fight their way out to the north they were totally destroyed.

The German tanks reached Allerborn that same afternoon, where they overwhelmed the rest of the American 2nd Tank Battalion, driving what was left of them back to Longvilly. Here confusion reigned. Trucks and men on foot were streaming westward; two regiments of American 105mm howitzers, the 73rd and 68th, were still in action and a scratch force of infantry, mostly Company G of the 110th Infantry, and four tank destroyers from the 630th Tank Destroyer Battalion, were dug in to protect the guns. Although shaken by the desperate fighting of the last two days and by the disintegration of their regiment in the face of five German divisions, these few men were still a formed body, capable of putting up some resistance. They were heartened in the evening when the leading tanks of Team Cherry reached the high ground just west of Longvilly. This was one of the three armoured infantry groups sent out by Col Roberts from his Combat Command B of the 10th Armored Division to delay the German advance on Bastogne and was made up of the Shermans of Company A, 3rd Tank Battalion, some light tanks, Company C of the 20th Armored Infantry and a reconnaissance platoon of the 90th Cavalry. Their commander, Lt-Col Cherry, now put his tanks and infantry in position to hold the high ground just west of Longvilly, established his own command post in the Chateau at Neffe and, leaving Capt William Ryerson in charge, drove back into Bastogne at about 11pm to report the situation to Col Roberts, passing a lot of vehicles from the 9th Armored Division in Mageret and on the road into Bastogne. A few minutes after he had passed through Mageret, the Germans seized the village, cutting the main road to Bastogne, shooting up the American trucks moving westwards and driving off the detachment

Left: Ogden Pleissner's painting of Bastogne. /*US War Dept*

Above: Pvt Margerum on an unusually peaceful road, December 1944./*US Army*

Right: Aerial view of Bastogne, showing clearly its importance as a road centre./*US Air Force*

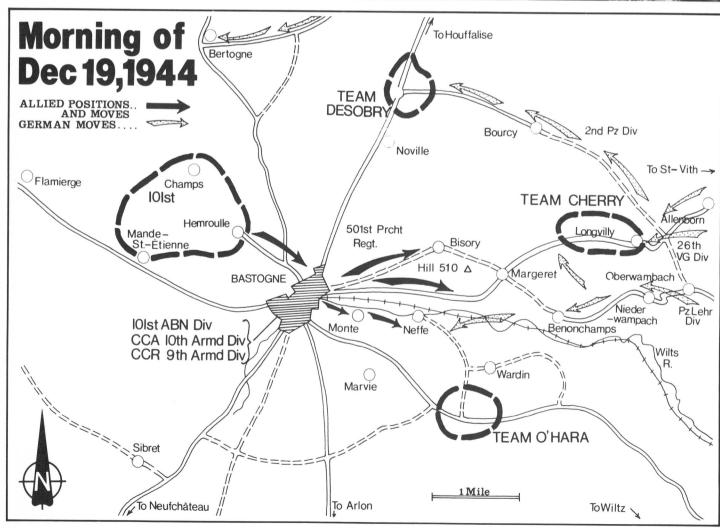

Morning of Dec 19, 1944

ALLIED POSITIONS..
AND MOVES ➡
GERMAN MOVES....

Bertogne

To Houffalise

TEAM DESOBRY

Noville

Bourcy

2nd Pz Div

To St-Vith →

Flamierge

Champs

101st

Hemroulle

Mande-
St-Étienne

TEAM CHERRY

Longvilly

Allenborn

26th VG Div

501st Prcht Regt.

Bisory

Hill 510 △

Margeret

Oberwampach

Pz Lehr Div

BASTOGNE

101st ABN Div
CCA 10th Armd Div
CCR 9th Armd Div

Monte

Neffe

Nieder-wampach

Benonchamps

Wilts R.

Marvie

Wardin

TEAM O'HARA

N

Sibret

To Neufchâteau

To Arlon

1 Mile

To Wiltz →

Left: A Sherman of the 9th Armored Division moving into Bastogne.
/US Army

Above: Olin Dows, a war artist, drew this picture of Neffe. The Chateau, where Col Cherry placed his command post is in the trees on the right. The 501st Parachute Infantry advanced from the left along the Bastogne road and deployed to their left, up the hill in the background. /US War Dept

Right: German Mark IV tanks moving forward./IWM

Below: Germans try to move a captured jeep, bogged down in the mud. /US Army

of US engineers holding the village. This was the leading battle-group of the Panzer Lehr Division and consisted of 15 Mark V tanks, a battalion of panzer grenadiers and a battery of guns.

At 11.40pm that same night the mixed bag of 9th Armored and 28th Infantry Division remnants in Longvilly began to withdraw westwards through the tanks and infantry of the Team Cherry, only to bump into the Germans in Mageret. During the rest of the night a solid traffic jam built up on the road between Longvilly and Mageret with jeeps, trucks, guns and tanks two and three abreast, struggling to escape westwards. Col Cherry got back to his command post in Neffe Chateau to find that he was now cut off from his tanks and infantry at Longvilly.

The Americans in Lallange, Allerborn and Longvilly had up to now been facing the full weight of the German 2nd Panzer Division, who were driving westwards in accordance with their orders to by-pass Bastogne to the north and press on to the Meuse. Just short of Longvilly their reconnaissance battalion swung north-west at Chifontaine on the road to Bourcy and Noville, leaving a screen of 88mm

guns to watch the Americans in Longvilly and to protect their own left flank. Coming up on the left of the 2nd Panzer was General Bayerlein's Panzer Lehr Division and by the afternoon of December 18th their leading battlegroup of 902nd Panzer Grenadier Regiment with 15 tanks, led by Bayerlein in person, had reached Niederwampach. Here they were delayed by the poor roads, which formed their route, and by the long columns of the 26th Volksgrenadier Division with their horse-drawn transport. The regiments of this infantry division had shown a high level of fitness in fighting for two days to breach the US lines and keeping up on foot with the tanks and half-tracks of the panzer divisions. Their divisional commander, Maj-Gen Kokott, was a scholarly and dignified officer, already 50 years old, but a calm, professional and resolute commander.

Lt-Gen Fritz Bayerlein was a capable staff officer and a vigorous personality, but now he began to show a surprising lack of drive. At Niederwampach that night of 18 December he accepted advice from a Belgian villager, that the side roads into Bastogne through Benonchamps were passable and his leading battalion of the 902nd Panzer Grenadiers with 15 Mark V Panthers set off at 10pm with their general in the leading tank. By 2am they had captured Mageret, where Bayerlein was shaken to hear that large numbers of American tanks were still east of him at Longvilly. He established a road block of three tanks and some infantry in Mageret facing east and at 5.30am the rest of his battlegroup moved on towards Neffe. Just east of the village the leading Panther went up on a mine, probably part of a Team Cherry road block, and while the mines were cleared, a company of panzer grenadiers reached Neffe Chateau, where a battle started with Col Cherry's command post and a platoon of the 35th Engineers. By 7am Bayerlein's tanks had reached Neffe station and here they waited for over an hour, an unexplained delay. When they moved forward again, they at once met machine gun fire and the village of Neffe was heavily shelled. This was the first contact with the US 101st Airborne Division and the fire was coming from the 1st Battalion of Col Julian Ewell's 501st Parachute Infantry, marching eastwards out of Bastogne, with orders to find and stop the enemy.

They now deployed rapidly to the left of the main road and their supporting artillery, Battery B of the 907th Glider Field Artillery, opened fire from their gun area just north-east of Bastogne. By noon Ewell's 2nd Battalion had come up and occupied Bizory, north of Neffe and his 3rd Battalion were moving into Mont to the south. Company I from the 3rd Battalion went on into Wardin and made contact with Team O'Hara, one of the 10th Armored Division blocking groups from Combat Command B. Here on the afternoon of this same day, 19 December, they were attacked by seven Mark IV tanks of the Panzer Lehr and the 39th Grenadier Regiment of the 26th Volksgrenadier Division and driven back to Mont. Capt Claude Wallace in Company I was killed and all their officers were among the 39 casualties suffered.

To the north at Bizory on the right of the Panzer Lehr, the 26th Volksgrenadier Division's reconnaissance battalion bumped into Maj Samuel Homan's 2nd Battalion of the 501st Parachute Infantry and were driven back with severe casualties. For the first time Bayerlein had met organised American resistance over a wide front. His troops and those of Gen Kokott's 26th Division were held up at Bizory, Neffe and Mont. Behind him, as he believed, there was a strong force of American tanks round Longvilly and he went back to Mageret in a depressed and pessimistic mood. He felt that before he tried to advance any further he must clear the enemy from his rear on the Mageret–Longvilly road. At 2pm that day, 19 December, the 901st Panzer Grenadier Regiment with an assault gun battalion in support and an artillery battalion firing from Renonchamps attacked this mass of American vehicles. The artillery of the 77th Grenadier Regiment in Oberwampach opened fire on the same target and from the north a half-dozen 88s from the 2nd Panzer Division in Chifontaine began to brew up Sherman after Sherman in that terrible traffic jam. In two hours every American vehicle and gun on the road between Longvilly and Mageret was wrecked and the road was marked by pillars of black smoke from burning trucks and tanks. In the middle of this hail of fire two attempts were made by the Americans of Team Cherry and 9th Armored to break through the German road block at Mageret. 18 men and two Sherman tanks put in an attack there at 3pm, which failed, and an hour later, while many men gave up the fight and took off across the fields to the north, 40 mixed infantry and dismounted tank crews tried again with two more tanks. Capt Ryerson and a few men finally reached Bizory and the 101st Division lines but Team Cherry's losses in the day's fighting were heavy – 175 men, 17 tanks and 17 half-tracks.

In Neffe Chateau Col Cherry and his few headquarters people held out all day against Bayerlein's panzer grenadiers. A platoon of American engineers left their positions in the chateau and were not seen again, quite contrary to the splendid record of the American engineer battalions in the whole of the Ardennes battle, but the rest of the chateau garrison moved from window to window, firing on their attackers and beating back every German attempt to storm the building. In the evening a platoon of the 501st Parachute Infantry's third battalion reached the chateau and as it was now on fire, Cherry and his men withdrew through the 501st back to Bastogne.

During the night of 18 December Col Lauchert's 2nd Panzer Division had swung north-westwards at Chifontaine on their way round the north of Bastogne. At 5.30am on 19 December the leading half-track of the reconnaissance battalion checked at a road-block in Bourcy, where an American voice shouted 'Halt' four times. The Germans shouted back and a shower of grenades from the ditches each side of the road made a butcher's shop of the leading German half-track, setting it on fire. Both sides started shooting in the darkness, and after 20 minutes the Germans withdrew. A little later, at first light, the Americans also fell back to Noville. These were men from Team Desobry, another of the task forces sent out by Col Roberts to block the main roads into Bastogne and to gain time for the deployment of the 101st Airborne Division. In command was Maj William Desobry, the commanding officer of the 20th Armored Infantry Battalion. With him was his own battalion, less Companies A and C, who were with the other two teams, Cherry and O'Hara. He also had 15 Shermans of Company B and a platoon of light tanks from the 3rd Tank Battalion, a platoon of Company C, 609th Tank Destroyers, a platoon of sappers from the 55th Armored Engineers and a platoon from the 90th Reconnaissance Squadron. Desobry's orders were to hold Noville, a village five miles north-east of Bastogne, overlooked by two ridges half a mile out to the south-east and north-west. His group reached Noville at 11pm on 18 December and three outposts were sent at once to establish road blocks at Bourcy on the main road to the east, on the Houffalize road to the north-east and on the road to Vaux to the north-west. Each outpost consisted of two Shermans and a platoon of armoured infantry. Through the night American stragglers poured through the road-blocks at Bourcy and on the Houffalize road in groups of three and four without arms or equipment or maps, low in morale and with only the vaguest news of the enemy's advance. Some were from the 28th Infantry Division, some from engineer and service units, others from the 9th Armored Division. Few would stay to fight, except for a platoon of armoured infantry from the 9th Armored Division, led by a lieutenant, who reached Noville in good order, gave Desobry clear and useful intelligence about the enemy and joined his task force for the battle to follow.

By 4.30 in the morning the flow of stragglers had ceased and the men at the road blocks listened in the dark for the sound of the enemy's tank tracks. At 5.30am the rattle of an approaching half-track alerted the Bourcy outpost and after their brisk fire-fight, they pulled back into Noville and reported to Maj Desobry. Twenty minutes later enemy tanks and infantry hit the block on the Houffalize road, knocking out both American tanks and after a fire-fight in the foggy darkness of early morning, these Americans too withdrew into Noville.

By now Desobry realised that he was astride the route forward of a large German force. At Noville he was in fact right on the main axis of the 2nd Panzer Division's advance. He and his men now blocked all the roads into the village; his infantry dug in just beyond the houses and tanks took up positions covering the road blocks. The morning was foggy, reducing visibility to no more than 30 yards. Suddenly at 8.30am two great Mark VI Tiger tanks clattered out of the fog from the north. At 30 yards range bazookas from the infantry fox-holes, a six-pounder anti-tank gun and a Sherman all fired together and in a minute both German tanks were total wrecks. An hour later tanks and infantry fired on the Americans in Noville from the west, the unexpected direction, and then at 10.30am the fog suddenly lifted, revealing 30 German tanks in the open ground between Noville and Bourcy. Capt Omar Billett, looking out of the upper window of the school-house, the command post of Company

Above: Wrecked American tanks and vehicles on the road between Longvilly and Mageret./*US Army*

B, 20th Armored Infantry, counted them carefully. 14 more German tanks came into view south of Vaux and as the visibility improved, they all began to plaster Noville with their 75mm guns. This was the 3rd Panzer Regiment, trying to blast a way through Noville for the 2nd Panzer Division.

By now a platoon of American tank destroyers had reached Noville and joined in the fire-fight. The German Mark IVs and Vs were clearly silhouetted against the lifting fog and nine of them were hit and destroyed, one of them by a lucky shot from an armoured car's 37mm pop-gun. A few of the German tanks got to within a hundred yards of the village, but the combination of the boggy ground and the effective fire from the American tanks and tank destroyers forced them to pull back and by 11.30am there was a lull in the noise and the shooting all round Noville.

While the battle was at its height, Desobry called Roberts on the radio and asked permission to withdraw to Foy, the next village to the south-west towards Bastogne. His voice at the microphone carried clearly to all the men in his command post and in minutes the word spread around the village, that they were getting out. Men began to filter back from the front-line fox-holes and Desobry and his officers had a struggle to stop the rot and to get the men back to their positions. In Bastogne Col Roberts hurried over to Gen McAuliffe's command post to tell him of Desobry's situation and on the way met Brig-Gen Higgins. It was 10.50am and as they stood, talking, the 1st Battalion, 506th Parachute Infantry marched by with Col Robert Sink and Lt-Col James LaPrade at their head. Higgins grabbed Sink and told him to send LaPrade's battalion straight on to Noville, while his 2nd and 3rd Battalions were to halt on the Noville road, just out of Bastogne, ready to act as a reserve. Roberts at once radio'ed to Desobry 'You can use your own judgment about withdrawing, but I'm sending you a battalion of paratroopers to reinforce you'. Desobry replied, 'I'll get ready to counter-attack as soon as possible'.

LaPrade's battalion reached Noville at noon. Due to their hurried move forward and their incomplete re-equipment after the fighting in Holland, the battalion was short of bazookas, mortar bombs and small arms ammunition and these were now brought up in jeeps by two quartermasters and dished out to the companies, as they marched. LaPrade and Desobry together made a rapid plan of action and at 2.30pm LaPrade's three parachute rifle companies attacked towards the high ground to the east and north of Noville, moving over the open fields, while Desobry's tanks and armoured infantry kept pace with them along the three roads out of the village. They met intense tank and machine gun fire from the ridges in front of them and the American armour pulled back into the village. The parachute Company A in the centre also withdrew, but Company B, astride the Bourcy road, fought their way forward, platoons moving by turns, in short rushes, covered by fire from the others. They reached the high ground, taking severe casualties on the way and held it until nightfall, beating off the German tanks with their bazookas. Then they withdrew to Noville under cover of darkness, leaving their dead on the ridge as witnesses of a fine example of resolute and skilful infantry taking on tanks.

Later that afternoon of 19 December, 2 Platoon of Company C from Templeton's 705th Tank Destroyers reached Noville with four of their tracked, self-propelled 90mm guns in time to join in the fire-fight and to knock out five of the 16 German tanks visible on the Bourcy ridge. Platoons of the 705th were now deployed with each of the parachute battalions round Bastogne and their powerful guns ably handled by Templeton's exceptionally well-trained men, seldom failed to take a heavy toll of the German armour throughout the battles of the next few days. Col Roberts, in Combat Command B of 10th Armored Division, both a theoretical and a practical expert

in armoured warfare and the principles of using armour in mass, had the flexibility of mind to appreciate how successful these tank destroyers were, shooting in pairs or even as single guns from stationary positions behind the cover of a house, a hedge or a bank and he urged his own tank crews to copy them. Brig-Gen Higgins came up in the afternoon, followed shortly afterwards by Col Sink, and placed LaPrade in command of all the troops in Noville. The defence was now reorganised with the parachute companies holding the perimeter of the village, dug in round the outer ring of houses and the tanks in the middle, as a mobile reserve. Four miles to the

south-west the 3rd Battalion 506th moved into Foy, and the 2nd Battalion to Luzery. The 502nd Parachute Infantry were already moving up to Recogne and the whole defence of Bastogne on the west and north was solidifying hourly. Through the evening and night of 19 December the artillery of the 2nd Panzer Division kept up a continuous bombardment of Noville and a constant series of patrols probed the American defences.

In LaPrade's command post, a house in the village, they moved a large cupboard to block the window, but an 88mm shell burst in the road outside. The shell fragments smashed through the cup-

Above left, left and above: The 506th Parachute Infantry moving through Bastogne on the Noville road on 19 December and passing vehicles of the 10th Armored Division./*US Army*

board, killed LaPrade and severely wounded Desobry in the head. Maj Robert Harwick, the executive offcer of the 1st Battalion, took over command of the whole force and Maj Charles Hustead now led the tanks.

So the fourth day of the Ardennes battle ended. Reports coming in to Gen Heinrich von Lüttwitz at his XLVII Panzer Korps command post were discouraging. The 2nd Panzer Division were held up at Noville, and both Panzer Lehr and the 26th Divisions had failed to out-flank or to penetrate the defences of Bastogne. These were now being rapidly consolidated by the 501st and 506th Parachute Infantry. All three German divisions had taken serious losses in men and tanks from the American artillery, tank and tank destroyer fire. Gens Bayerlein and Kokott now urged Lüttwitz to turn the whole strength of his corps against Bastogne and he repeated this request to Gen Manteuffel at Fifth Panzer Army. Manteuffel refused to agree and stressed the need for the 2nd Panzer Division to press on north of Bastogne to the Meuse, while Panzer Lehr was to move south of the town, leaving part of their armour to help the 26th Volksgrenadier Division capture Bastogne.

The next morning, 20 December, was again foggy and visibility was made worse by smoke and dust. The Germans looking down at Noville from the high ground on the east and north and the Americans in the village, peering into the fog, had been marching and fighting for three days and nights and they were all very tired. Suddenly at 7.30am in the half-light, two Mark IV tanks, driving fast down the Houffalize road, got right into Noville. A Sherman tank, with Sergeant Lesniak in command, fired at them and a flurry of bazooka bombs burst on them from the parachute soldiers in slit trenches beside the road. Both German tanks were knocked out and their crews killed. Soon afterwards a series of uncoordinated tank and infantry attacks came in through the fog and smoke all round the village and were beaten back. Then at 10 o'clock the fog cleared, revealing 15 German tanks, followed by infantry, advancing from the south. The American tank destroyers, firing from between the village houses, destroyed four of them, but a big Mark VI Tiger

crashed into the village, right up to Capt Omar Billet's school-house command post. He opened the door, found himself looking down the barrel of an 88, at five yards range, closed the door again and said 'This is no place for my pistol'. 20 yards away Sergeant Lesniak found that his Sherman turret was jammed, but he manoeuvred his tank round and fired three rounds at the Tiger. They bounced off, the Tiger reversed, ran over a jeep, fouled one track, slewed round, collided with an American half-track and turned over onto its side. The crew baled out and ran for it, disappearing in the smoke, fog and general confusion, without a shot being fired at them. In the Tiger the radio went on nattering in German, until Hustead's tank crews destroyed the Tiger with a thermite grenade – and later earned a sharp rebuke from Col Roberts for not bringing it back to Bastogne. However this was excusable, as casualties among tank crews now meant that one Sherman could not be manned. Two parachute soldiers got into it and drove it, until the tank was hit and they were both killed later that day. No less than eight of the remaining Shermans were now out of gun ammunition.

While the 2nd Panzer Division were battering at Noville, two companies of the 78th Grenadier Regiment, supported by four tanks attacked the 3rd Battalion 506th in Foy and the battalion pulled back to the high ground just south of the village.

Gens McAuliffe and Higgins, Col Roberts and Col Sink felt by now, that there was little point in holding on to Noville with the probable loss of everyone in the village. Orders were radio'ed to Majs Harwick and Hustead to break out to the south and both the 3rd/506th near Foy, and the 3rd/502nd on their left were told to attack north to help the Noville's garrison's withdrawal. On reaching Recogne Lt-Col John Stopka's 3rd/502nd were ordered to dig in and hold there, while the 3rd/506th continued to move north, back into Foy.

In Noville Harwick had 50 wounded to look after, but enough tanks and vehicles to lift everyone, except for Company C of the 506th, with three tanks as advance guard and Company B and four tank destroyers as rear-guard. Between these two groups on foot were the rest of the tanks and the vehicles with the wounded. At 1.15pm they blew up their remaining ammunition dump and set off down the road to Foy and Bastogne, just as the fog closed in again. About 500 yards short of Foy, Maj James Duncan, thinking his driver's sudden gesture meant he was wounded, slammed on

Above left: A German Mark IV tank knocked out by the 506th in Foy. Passing it is a half-track of the 6th Armored Division during their advance through Foy in mid-January./*US Army*

Left: The village street in Foy after the battle./*US Army*

Above: Lt-Col Julian Ewell, commanding the 501st Parachute Infantry – now a retired Lt-Gen, living in Maclean, Virginia.

the brakes of his half-track. The one behind crashed into him, a traffic jam developed, the enemy opened fire from each side of the road and at the same time the noise of battle south of Foy intensified, where the 3rd/506th were coming northwards. Two Shermans in the jam were hit and flamed, a tank destroyer backed suddenly to avoid a Sherman and crushed a jeep. Another Sherman, on fire and with its turret blown off, now blocked the road completely. In the fifth Sherman there was no driver and none available amongst the other tank crews and after cursing the tank men for a lot of idle scroungers, three parachute soldiers climbed in and drove it off the road and round the blockage. Behind this confusion the rearguard company and their tank destroyers moved off the road to the right and reached Foy, after some confused fighting in which Pvt Thomas Gallagher in one of the tank destroyers with two parachute soldiers as his crew, burned up one Mark IV tank and chased off another.

Eventually most of them reached the lines of the 3rd/506th south of Foy, but several jeep-loads of wounded were captured, including Maj Desobry. His team finally reassembled in Bastogne with four tanks left out of the 15 with which he had started. The 1st Battalion 506th Parachute Infantry had lost 13 officers and 199 soldiers in Noville, including their colonel killed. The 2nd Panzer Division had lost a lot of men and between 20 and 30 tanks in the 3rd Panzer Regiment, including three Tigers, but much more seriously, they were now 48 hours behind schedule.

On the same day, 20 December, the 902nd Panzer Grenadiers attacked Neffe, but were beaten back with heavy loss by the fire of the 501st Parachute Infantry, the 705th's tank destroyers and the American artillery. The 78th Grenadiers probed in towards the 506th round Foy again without success and in the south-west the 2nd Battalion 327th Glider Infantry came up to relieve the 35th

Engineers in Marvie in time to join with the 10th Armored Division's Team O'Hara in completely destroying the leading company of the 901st Panzer Grenadiers and four Mark IV tanks in a furious fight for Marvie village.

In these three days, 18, 19 and 20 December, American losses in men, tanks, guns and vehicles had been heavy. Combat Command R, 9th Armored Division, had ceased to exist, over 60 tanks had been lost in both 9th and 10th Armored Divisions and the 506th's 1st Battalion had been cut in half. But Gen von Lüttwitz's XLVII Panzer Korps were now three days behind schedule. His divisions had suffered severely in men and tanks and his troops had now been marching and fighting continuously for five days. Worse still from his point of view, the 101st Airborne Division, Combat Command B, 10th Armored Division, Templeton's 705th Tank Destroyers and the American artillery had had time to reach Bastogne and to establish the all-round defence of the town. The American armoured infantry and artillery task-forces, rushed forward by Gens Middleton and McAuliffe to delay the German advance, had done their job well.

As soon as Gen McAuliffe and Lt-Col Kinnard had seen Gen Middleton at 4pm on 18 December, they went off to look for an assembly area for their division west of Bastogne round Mande St Etienne and Flamierge. This was a good choice, since it was well to the west and clear of the traffic jams in Bastogne. From it the regiments could move straight to their assigned sectors of the defence. At 8pm the last trucks of the division left their base area at Mourmelon in France and at the same time, the divisional artillery commander, Col Thomas Sherburne, learning that his general had gone on to Bastogne, posted a military policeman at a vital crossroads west of the town, with orders to turn all 101st traffic down the right road.

At 10pm Lt-Col Julian Ewell, commanding the 501st Parachute Infantry, a tall, lean professional soldier with a sardonic sense of humour, reached the divisional command post. He had commanded the 3rd Battalion of the regiment in Normandy and at Eindhoven and by chance had spent a week's leave in Bastogne the previous October. McAuliffe said to him 'Ewell, move out along this road . . .' pointing on the map to the main road to Neffe and Longvilly, 'At 6 o'clock, make contact, attack and clean up the situation'. Ewell replied 'Yes, Sir', saluted, turned about and left the command post. By midnight his regiment were all in the divisional assembly area and he gave out his orders to his battalion and artillery commanders, ending with the words 'Take it slow and easy. I don't want you to try to beat the enemy to death'.

At 6am on 19 December the 501st marched east out of Bastogne, led by a reconnaissance troop and Maj Raymond Bottomly's 1st Battalion. With them went seven six-pounder anti-tank guns of Battery B, 81st Airborne Anti-Aircraft Battalion and a forward observer from Lt-Col Clarence Nelson's 907th Glider Field Artillery. Their guns went into action west of Bastogne with B Battery forward in a field just east of the town. The fog was thick and at about 7am Ewell found that his leading battalion had turned right in error onto the road to Marvie, but he was able to turn them back quickly onto the right road. There were only 20 maps for the whole regiment and Ewell's previous knowledge of the country around Bastogne came in useful here and in the days that followed. They marched through a countryside of grassy fields, over long, gently rolling ridges, running from north to south, topped by dense forests of pine trees and dotted with clusters of farm buildings.

At 9am the leading section came under machine gun fire from the houses on the western edge of Neffe and the 1st Battalion deployed rapidly to the left of the main road. The artillery forward observer called for fire and in minutes the guns of the 907th were plastering Neffe village. Julian Ewell came forward to reconnoitre the ground and by noon his second battalion were moving left into Bizory with orders to advance and seize Mageret. On Hill 501 they met the reconnaissance battalion of the 26th Volksgrenadiers and drove them back in a brisk fire fight. At the same time George Griswold's 3rd Battalion marched south to Mont and Wardin, where

Top: Survivors from the 110th Infantry reach Bastogne and are organised into Team SNAFU, as a general reserve./*US Army*

Above: Negro troops, probably of the 771st Artillery, moving westwards out of Bastogne, as transport of the 101st Airborne Division enter the town./*US Army*

they clashed with the Panzer Lehr Division. During this first day of action stragglers were still coming through the 501st from the 28th Infantry Division and from the 9th Armored. Most of them were without arms and in defeatist mood and little attempt was made to stop them. Back in Bastogne Col Roberts set up a network of military police posts on all the roads out of the town to catch these stragglers, and by the evening of this same day, 19 December, 250 men had been assembled, given a hot meal and organised as Team SNAFU. As the battle went on, these men were sent out as reinforcements to the various units of the garrison. In contrast to many other units the 109th Field Artillery withdrew through the 501st in good order with nine of their guns and attached themselves to the

907th Glider Artillery. Another regiment, the 73rd Armored Field Artillery, were rumbling westwards through Bastogne on 19 December, past Col Roberts, standing in the road, watching them go, when he suddenly realised what he was losing, grabbed their commanding officer and sent them into action. The 58th Armored Field Artillery also joined the gun areas, building up west of the town and two days later, the 771st Battalion with their 155mm Long Toms were conscripted into McAuliffe's Bastogne garrison. That night seven Sherman tanks and a platoon of armoured infantry from the 9th Armored joined Sammie Homan's 2nd/501st. Homan's battalion was further strengthened early on the 20th by the arrival of Lt Frederick Mallon's 2nd Platoon, Company B, 705th Tank Destroyers. These four guns were soon in action, as a Mark IV and a Mark V with two assault guns attacked Bizory with the 2nd Battalion, 76th Grenadier Regiment. One of the American tank destroyers was hit and knocked out, another damaged its gun against a wall, but the other two destroyed both the German tanks and one of the assault guns. The American artillery brought down a heavy concentration of fire and the German grenadiers faded away.

The rest of the day was quiet, until at 7pm the Germans opened up with guns and mortars all along the front of the 501st from Bizory on the north to Mont in the south. The 1st Battalion reported German attacks from Neffe and all the American artillery in Bastogne, by now the best part of eleven battalions, fired the heaviest weight of shells of the whole siege. A Mark V and a Mark VI tank were destroyed and a whole company of the 902nd Panzer Grenadiers were wiped out. At Mont the 3rd Battalion had also been reinforced by four tank destroyers from the 705th under Lt Robert Andrews and for three and a half hours that evening they were continuously in action, as the 901st Panzer Grenadiers tried to capture the village. The attack failed and next morning the daylight showed long lines of German dead, caught at the cattle fences, which criss-crossed the fields in front of Mont, with three wrecked assault guns amongst them.

While the 501st was under pressure from the Panzer Lehr Division on this evening of 20 December, a battalion of the 77th Grenadier Regiment from the German 26th Division made a bold attempt to penetrate by night down the road and railway from the

Top: A post from the 501st Parachute Infantry with a bazooka, watching the road eastwards out of Bastogne./*US Army*

Above: Olin Dows' drawing of the scene of the action between Neffe and Mont. This view from the outskirts of Neffe shows the enemy preparing to attack the 501st's 3rd Battalion positions on the hill in the left background. Mont is in the centre distance and the fences below the pine trees mark where the lines of German dead lay./*US War Dept*

north-east into the gap between the American 501st and 506th Parachute Infantry. This could have been a serious threat to the American positions, but some vigorous patrolling by companies from these two regiments cut off the Germans and some 235 of them were killed or captured. This was the last of the German attempts to attack Bastogne from the east through the 501st and 506th.

During the fighting of these two days, Team O'Hara from Combat Command B, 10th Armored Division, one of the three task forces sent out on 18 December to delay the German advance, had

been established in a defensive position on the Bastogne to Wiltz road about three quarters of a mile east of Marvie. At 6.45am on 20 December they were shelled and when the fog lifted they saw German engineers working to remove their road block. The 420th Armored Artillery dropped a concentration on them and killed two of the German sappers. Early that same morning Lt-Col Roy Inman's 2nd Battalion, 327th Glider Infantry, marched through Bastogne with orders from Col Bud Harper, their regimental commander, to relieve an engineer outpost in Marvie and to hold the village. They got there at 9am and after contacting O'Hara and reconnoitring the village, Inman put his battalion into a position from Marvie village on the left to the Bastogne-Remoifosse road on his right. Team O'Hara's medium tanks were a few hundred yards to the north and his light tanks were just behind Marvie village.

Harper had just left the battalion on his way back to his command post in Bastogne and was on the hill behind Marvie, when the 901st Panzer Grenadiers attacked. Under cover of heavy mortar fire, four German tanks and six half-tracks full of infantry came out of the woods south-east of Marvie and moved towards the village, firing as they came at the American light tanks. O'Hara's Shermans, hidden in the woods on the German right flank, held their fire, until the range was 700 yards. Then they hit and destroyed two German tanks. A third turned and trundled back into the woods, but the fourth tank got right into Marvie village, where it was burned up by an American bazooka. The German half-tracks also drove into the village, where the infantry dismounted and grappled with the American glider troops, dug in among the houses, in some furious hand to hand fighting.

On the hill behind the village Col Harper had stopped his jeep to watch the battle. The engineers, relieved by the 2nd/327th were moving back to Bastogne, as they had been ordered to do, and a glider mortar platoon from an orchard in rear of the houses saw them go, heard and felt the shelling and the noise of battle and thought everyone was pulling out. They fell in behind the engineers, only to be stopped on the track by their own regimental commander and sent back to their positions. Harper radio'ed to McAuliffe, that the situation looked serious, but by 1pm Marvie was cleared of Germans, 20 of them were prisoners, 30 were dead and the glider battalion had lost five men killed and 15 wounded.

That night, 20 December, the temperature fell sharply and it began to snow. Shelter and warmth became as important as fields of fire and villages and farms acquired a new tactical significance. The German plan was still to send on the 2nd Panzer Division round the north of Bastogne towards the Meuse and by 20 December they were through Noville. They were held up all day at Tenneville by Company B, 3rd/327th Glider Infantry and made no progress on 21 and 22 December, partly because of a shortage of

fuel and partly 'held up by a road block'. Gen von Lüttwitz went forward himself to find out why they were so delayed and found the road-block unmanned and no Americans in sight. He began to take down the logs himself in a fury and then went back to relieve the leading regimental commander and to order his court martial for cowardice.

South of Bastogne the Germans were trying to outflank the Americans to find a way into the town from 20 December onwards. That afternoon, while the Panzer Lehr was hammering at the 501st in Bizory, Neffe and Mont and at the 2nd/327th in Marvie, Gen Kokott's 26th Reconnaissance Battalion and his 39th Grenadier Regiment drove westwards through Lutremange, Villers-la-Bonne-Eau, Hompré and Sibret. The 39th reached the high ground a kilometre north of Remoifosse and the wood north of Assenois, where they were checked by the American 327th Glider Infantry and the 326th Engineers. The German 26th Reconnaissance Battalion got as far as Chenogne that night and were in contact with the 327th in Mande Ste Etienne next morning, 21 December. On the previous day their general, Kokott, had a narrow escape, when his command half-track was hit by a shell in Wardin, which killed all the men inside. Kokott in the road near-by was hurled against the church wall and badly bruised and shaken. Now at 2am on 21 December he had recovered and began to make fresh plans for his task of capturing Bastogne, while the Panzer Lehr Division pushed on to the west. One of Bayerlein's regiments, the 901st Panzer Grenadiers, were left facing Marvie, and put under Kokott's command. In his command post at Bra news reached him of the advance on his left of the German 5th Parachute Division and the number of Americans he had seen withdrawing in front of his troops led him to believe that the garrison of Bastogne was disintegrating. During the next two days Kokott's 26th Volksgrenadier Division took up positions right round Bastogne with the 78th Grenadier Regiment on the north-east facing the American 506th Parachute Infantry, the 77th Regiment on the north-west opposite the 502nd and the 327th Glider Infantry, the 39th Regiment and the 26th Reconnaissance Battalion to the south-west and the 901st Panzer Grenadiers in front of Marvie in the south-east.

On the American side Harry Kinnard's original plan for the deployment of the 101st Airborne Division and its supporting units had put the main strength to the east, where the threat was most immediate. On the south and west the 327th Glider Infantry were stretched out from the 2nd Battalion in Marvie in the south through

the 1st Battalion astride the Bastogne-Neufchateau road to Lt-Col Ray Allen's 3rd Battalion's positions near Mande Ste Etienne on the west. In the gap between the 1st and 3rd Battalions were the gun areas for most of the American artillery just north of Senonchamps. To protect them, Lt-Col Barry Browne, the commanding officer of the 420th Armored Field Artillery, was given a scratch force of 14 tanks and 200 infantry, mostly from the 9th Armored Division. Nearby were the 155mm guns of the negro 755th Field Artillery with part of the 333rd Artillery attached to them, and closer in to Bastogne were the Airborne artillery battalions, three armed with the little 75mm howitzer and one with the short barrelled 105mm.

Firing with them were the remnants of the 109th and 73rd regiments from the 9th Armored and 28th Divisions.

During the night of 20 December and the morning of the 21st, Oberst Kunkel with the 26th Reconnaissance Battalion captured Sibret and advanced north towards Senonchamps, driving before them the two American regiments of 155mm guns and capturing some of the guns. Col Browne's scratch force now appeared on the scene and, aided by Maj Pyle and the Quad .50s of the 796th Anti-Aircraft Battalion, halted Kunkel's battlegroup and covered the escape northwards of most of the medium gunners.

For most of the next day, 22 December, there was a lull in the

99

fighting round Bastogne, except in the west, where the Panzer Lehr Division had reached Tillet and had surrounded the American 58th Armored Field Artillery. The gunners held out for most of the day, firing their self-propelled 105mm howitzers over open sights at the German tanks, but by the evening they were overrun and seven of their eight guns were captured. Near Senonchamps Col Browne, Maj Pyle and Maj Van Kleef with their tanks and infantry fought off the Kunkel battlegroup all day, while the divisional artillery fired round the whole perimeter.

In Bastogne the afternoon of 22 December was perhaps Gen McAuliffe's most anxious time. Although all his guns were sited to fire round 360°, ammunition was running out. The guns were now rationed to 10 rounds a day and the artillery forward observers, strictly limited to firing on serious attacks only, watched with frustration, as the German columns streamed west on both sides of Bastogne in clear view and easy range. Col Sherburne, the 101st's artillery commander, lied cheerfully to everyone about his serious ammunition state, but told his gunners: 'if you see 400 Germans in a 100-yard area with their heads up you can fire artillery at them – but not more than two rounds per gun!'

All round the perimeter of Bastogne on that morning of December 22nd the men in the slit trenches had been taking advantage of the lull in the fighting to wash and shave. At noon a German major, a lieutenant and two soldiers appeared on the road from Remoifosse, carrying a large white flag. They were allowed to approach the positions of Company F, 327th Glider Infantry, where they told T/Sgt Oswald Butler and S/Sgt Carl Dickinson and Pvt Ernest Premetz, a medical orderly, that they were 'parlementaires.' The two officers were blindfolded and taken to Lt Smith, the weapons platoon commander, and by him to Capt James Adams at Company F headquarters. In no time at all the rumour spread that the Germans had come in to surrender. Leaving the two German officers at the company headquarters, Col Harper and Maj Alvin James took their written message to Col Ned Moore, the chief of staff at divisional headquarters. The message called for the surrender of Bastogne under threat of 'complete destruction'; appealed to the 'well-known American humanity'; and gave two hours for consideration; a major attack would otherwise begin at 1500 hours. Ned Moore took it in to Gen McAuliffe with whom was his operations officer, Harry Kinnard and several other staff officers. McAuliffe asked what was in the paper and when told its contents, he said 'Aw, Nuts'. Then he sat down with a pencil and paper, saying 'Well, I don't know what to tell them.' He asked for some ideas and Kinnard said: 'That first remark of yours could be hard to beat'. McAuliffe asked what he meant, was reminded of his first words and the staff applauded. Harper was called in and given the reply in writing and told to see it was delivered. 'I will do it myself', he replied, 'It will be a lot of fun'. McAuliffe told him not to go into the German lines and Harper went back to his Company F. There he told the still blindfolded Germans 'I have the American Commander's reply. It is written. I will stick it in your hand'. The German asked in a patronizing way 'Is the reply negative or affirmative? If it is the latter, I will negotiate further'. With some heat Harper replied 'It is decidedly not affirmative and if you continue this foolish attack, your losses will be tremendous'.

They all got into Harper's jeep and returned to platoon headquarters, where the two German soldiers were waiting. The blindfolds were removed and Harper said to the English-speaking officer, 'If you don't understand what "Nuts" means, in plain English it is the same as "Go to Hell" – and I will tell you something else, if you continue to attack, we will kill every goddam German who tries to break into this city'. The Germans saluted and one of them said 'We will kill many Americans. This is war'. Harper replied, 'On your way, Bud, and good luck to you' and as the four Germans walked away down the road, he wished he had left out the good luck bit. It was 10 minutes to 2 o'clock.

Nothing happened at 3pm and two feeble attacks on Company F later that evening were easily repulsed. The news of this offer and McAuliffe's reply spread rapidly through Bastogne, causing a lot of amusement and a good deal of pride. On the German side, when it became known later on, there was considerable resentment and disapproval of the whole idea and the author of it, Gen Von Lüttwitz, agreed after the war, that he had made an error of judgment and had misread the American mood and morale. It certainly gave the Americans a marvellous story and one which added to the publicity surrounding the 'Battered Bastards of Bastogne'.

That same afternoon a radio message from VIII Corps confirmed that the 4th Armored Division was fighting its way up from the south to relieve Bastogne and half an hour later another message warned of a pathfinder parachute drop west of the town at 4pm, to be followed by a supply drop at 8pm. Icing problems, however, caused both to be cancelled and the pathfinders finally landed at 9.35am on the next day, 23 December, followed 90 minutes later by 16 Dakotas, dropping supplies. By 4.06pm 241 aircraft had dropped 144 tons of supplies and by 5pm all the stores had been shifted to unit dumps by jeeps, commandeered from each regiment, in a shuttle organised by Col Kohls, Maj Butler and Capt Matheson. The supply problem was not yet solved, however. Too much .50 cal ammunition had been dropped and not enough .30cal for machine guns and rifles, 75mm shell for the airborne howitzers or 76mm for the tank destroyers. Next day 160 aircraft dropped a further 100 tons, but there was still only enough food for one more day and only 445gal of fuel.

On Christmas Day the weather deteriorated, but 11 Waco gliders were able to land with a field surgical team and 10 loads of fuel. Finally on 26 December, 289 aircraft dropped their loads, mostly made up of artillery ammunition, Each wave of transport aircraft came in escorted by P-47 fighters, who usually went on to attack targets round the town. Although the first day's fly-in met little flak, aircraft on the following days met a good deal of 20mm and machine gun fire and suffered some losses. They flew in steadily, however, at low level, all the drops were accurate and the daily spectacle of these massive formations of aircraft raised the morale of the Americans in Bastogne and depressed the spirits of the watching Germans.

A series of photographs showing the air drop of supplies to the 101st Airborne Division in Bastogne: *Left:* The pathfinders set up their radar beacon, on which the transport aircraft can home./*US Army*; *Below:* C47 Douglas Dakotas of the US 9th Troop Carrier Command approaching Bastogne./*US Air Force*; *Bottom:* A 'quad 50' crew near the drop zone watch the C47's approach./*US Army*

Left: The supplies go down./*US Air Force*
Bottom left: Another view of the drop from
a cemetery in Bastogne; *Right:* Clearing the
drop zone; *Below:* A C-47, hit by 20mm
anti-aircraft fire, force-landed near Bastogne;
Bottom: A wrecked Waco glider near Bastogne,
stripped by souvenir hunters.
/*US Army* (2); *IWM*

Above left: Men of the 101st collecting rations./*US Army*

Left: Bomb damage in Bastogne./*US Army*

Above: Inside the 501st's aid station in Bastogne, the main hospital for casualties during the siege./*US Army*

The divisional and regimental supply staffs had improvised as best they could. Flour, lard, salt and coffee had been found in an abandoned VIII Corps warehouse and a bakery began making flapjacks. Potatoes, poultry and cattle were requisitioned from farms and in another abandoned store they found 450lb of coffee, 600lb of sugar and a stack of Ovaltine, most of which was kept for the wounded. A civilian store produced margarine, jam, flour and 2000 canvas sacks, which were cut up into overshoes. The wounded were a continuing problem, because the 101st Division's field hospital, Lt-Col Gill's 326th Medical Company, had been captured on 19 December at their crossroads site near the Bois de Herbaimont west of Flamierge, by the leading elements of the 2nd Panzer Division. The 501st Parachute Infantry's aid station in Bastogne took over as the main hospital and most of the casualties were evacuated by the 429th Medical Collecting Unit at Jodenville in five ambulances and two half-tracks until the road was cut on 21 December by the German 26th Reconnaissance Battalion. Some blankets and stretchers were found in Bastogne, but there was a shortage of surgeons, surgical instruments and penicillin. In the confused situation west of the town on 20 and 21 December two convoys of the division's quartermaster and ordnance companies were attacked and scattered, although Capt John Patterson managed to get through to Bastogne with two trucks and 500gal

of fuel and then went out again to search in vain for the rest. Just before the roads westward were cut by the Germans, S/Sgt Vincent Morgan from the 907th Glider Field Artillery with five trucks covered 75 miles round Neufchateau looking for ammunition, eventually returning with 1,500 rounds of M2 105mm, which could be fired in emergency from his regiment's short M3 guns.

Until the town was finally surrounded by German units on the night of 20 December the command situation was confused, in that the 101st Airborne Division and Combat Command B, 10th Armored Division were working together with no clear ruling as to who was in command. Col Roberts, with a lifetime of experience in armour, considered the airborne troops incapable of handling tanks properly, while Brig-Gen McAuliffe made it clear he was not putting himself or his division under a mere Combat Team. There was a feeling, too, amongst the tank crews, that they were doing all the fighting and the same belief in the parachute and glider battalions. Gen Middleton now clarified the situation by making McAuliffe overall commander of the Bastogne garrison. Robert's command post was already established close to McAuliffe's and he now spent most of his time with McAuliffe. Lt-Col Templeton from the 705th Tank Destroyers did the same and a close-knit sense of purpose and of teamwork spread downwards from the command level to all ranks.

Tanks, tank destroyers and airborne infantry and guns learned from each other and eventually by Christmas Eve the garrison were regrouped on a plan worked out by Harry Kinnard into combined teams of all arms, based on the four infantry regiments of the 101st. The 501st Parachute Infantry, Team O'Hara's tanks and a platoon of the 705th's tank destroyers formed one team; the 506th and a platoon of tank destroyers another; the 502nd, two platoons of

tank destroyers and Team Anderson a third; and the 327th Glider Infantry a fourth with the 326th Airborne Engineers, two platoons of the 9th Armored Engineers and four platoons of the 705th Tank Destroyers. Protecting the gun areas in the west was Team Browne with the 420th Armored Field Artillery and the same mixed group of tanks and infantry as before. Lt-Col Browne was mortally wounded by a shell on Christmas Eve and Maj Roberts took over the team, which Browne had led so well.

The fog, rain and low cloud of the first few days kept both the Luftwaffe and the Allied air forces on the ground and enabled the German armoured formations to roll forward without fear of air attack. Their inability to clear the road nets round St Vith and Bastogne and to widen the narrow penetrations achieved by the 1st SS Panzer Division in the north and the XLVII Panzer Korps in the south, led to a series of traffic jams up to 10 miles long, as the follow-up German infantry and panzer units struggled to get forward on too few roads and on tracks, which were rapidly becoming quagmires. Now on 23 December the day broke fine and clear. Four days before, Capt James Parker and Sgt Frank Hotard of the United States IX Air Force had reached Bastogne and had set up as a forward air controller with one radio set in a tank and another in a jeep, ready to talk to Allied aircraft. By now all the units of the Bastogne garrison were connected by telephone with good lateral, alternative lines and their forward, defended localities were clearly defined. At 10 o'clock Parker was warned by radio that strike aircraft were on the way and after contacting them by radio he brought them in at low level onto enemy targets west and north-west of Bastogne. He would pick them up some miles out and direct them to a clearly visible and distinctive crossroads or rail junction and thence on a bearing and distance to their target.

Snow had been falling for two days and the columns of German tanks and vehicles stood out clearly. Tracks in the snow pointed to vehicles hidden in the pine forests and the pilots had a field-day. One of them described it as better than the slaughter of the Falaise Gap and for the next four days the town was ringed with the black and white columns of smoke from German vehicles on fire and pine forests, set ablaze by napalm. 250 aircraft sorties a day answered calls for support from the troops in Bastogne with an average time-lag of only 20 minutes.

On this same fine day, 23 December, Gen Kokott was concerned as how best to obey his recently emphasised orders to capture Bastogne. In the west his 39th Grenadier Regiment pushed back the 3rd Battalion 327th Glider Infantry to the high ground west of Champs and Grandes-Fanges but got no further. Kunkel's battlegroup tried once more to drive the American artillery out of their gun areas near Senonchamps in the south-west, but was held

up again by Team Browne and some intense shelling. In the southeast the 901st Panzer Grenadiers attacked Marvie for the second time and this was to be the main German effort of the day.

At 5.25pm, the 2nd Battalion 327th in and round Marvie were heavily shelled and mortared for 10 minutes. Under the cover of this fire, tanks and infantry in white snow-suits moved forward to attack and by 6.40pm the platoon of Company G, forward on Hill 500, was surrounded. Four German tanks from this hill began pounding Marvie village. One of Team O'Hara's half-tracks, towing a six-pounder, retreating from Hill 500 in the gathering darkness was knocked out in error by the glider troops in the village and all the crew killed. Two German tanks, following close behind it, were blocked by the burning vehicle, but the German infantry swarmed into the village, shouting as they came. At 7pm Colonel Harper called Lt Stanley Morrison and his 98 men of Company G on Hill 500 'What is your situation?' Morrison replied, 'We are

Top left: A Lightning taxies out. /*US Air Force*

Above left: A Lightning coming in to land. /*US Air Force*

Left: . . . and another skids on landing, crashing into a fuel truck./*US Air Force*

Above: P-47 Thunderbolts of the 365th Fighter Bomber Group take-off to attack German targets round Bastogne. /*US Air Force*

Right: Bombs for a P-47./*US Air Force*

Above left: German vehicles near Houffalize, destroyed by Allied air attack./*US Air Force*

Left: An American jeep, a German Mark V Panther and a Mark IV tank, knocked out by air attack in front of the US Third Army.

Above: A 9th Air Force officer, Capt James Lloyd, beside a German assault gun, destroyed by air attack./*US Air Force*

Right: Lt William Simpkins sets a German vehicle on fire with .50cal machine gun fire. /*US Air Force*

Far right: Lt Richard Law does the same for an ammunition truck./*US Air Force*

56015 A.C.

56002 A.C.

still holding out, but it looks like they have us.' Then the line went dead, as the panzer grenadiers and 12 tanks overwhelmed the platoon.

By 8pm the German infantry in the south end of Marvie village were being reinforced by more tanks. The executive officer of the 2nd Battalion, Maj Galbraith, called regimental headquarters for tank support and was told by Col Harper 'You call O'Hara on your radio and say it is the commanding general's order, that two Sherman tanks move into Marvie at once and take up a defensive position.' This worked and two tanks arrived in time to strengthen the American infantry, fighting in the village. A German assault gun was brewed up at close range by Pvt Osterberg with a bazooka, a feat which won him the Distinguished Service Cross, but the situation began to look critical.

At 9.45pm a platoon of 40 men from Company A of the 501st, led by Capt Stanfield Stach, arrived to join the fight and soon afterwards Batteries D and E of the 81st Anti-Aircraft Battalion and part of Team Cherry drove up from Bastogne, as reinforcements. With close protection from Stach's men the 12 Quad .50s formed a line of defence on the high ground west of Marvie, as a back-stop for the 2nd Battalion. On the right flank Lt Smith's and Sgt Butler's glider platoons astride the Arlon road held their positions in the face of heavy and continuous attack, but could not stop two Mark IV tanks, which drove on right into Bastogne, before they were finally knocked out. As the light grew the next morning, the American infantry, dug in among the houses in Marvie, found they could pick off the less well protected Germans in the south end of the village and by 9am the village was clear and the situation restored. American aircraft struck repeatedly at the retreating men and vehicles of the 901st Panzer Grenadiers, but the effect on American feelings was spoiled, when at 1.40pm six P-47 fighter bombers attacked Marvie with six 500lb bombs and machine gun fire, in spite of a widespread and hurried display of cerise recognition points. To the rage and astonishment of the Americans in the village a similar attack came in again at 4.45pm and reduced considerably the ground troops' confidence in their air support.

While this attack was starting on the previous afternoon, 23 December, Gen Kokott received the serious news, that the German 5th Parachute Division on his southern flank were falling back in front of the United States 4th Armored Division, driving up from the south. He sent five of his precious Mark VI Tiger tanks down through Clochimont to help them. He had also watched the American supply drop over Bastogne with some misgiving, but to balance all this he now heard from Gen Manteuffel in person that the 9th Panzer and 15th Panzer Grenadier Divisions had been released from OKW reserve to Army Group B and that one battle-group from the latter, based on the 115th Panzer Grenadier Regiment under Oberst Wolfgang Maucke, would be allotted to him for the capture of Bastogne. This was a powerful unit, veterans from the Italian front and made up of three panzer grenadier battalions, a reconnaissance battalion, two armoured field artillery battalions, a company of assault guns and 17 tanks: but they were still many miles away to the east.

Gen Kokott decided to attack this time from the north-west and ordered Maucke to bring his battlegroup round to Flamierge. While Maucke attacked towards Flamizoulle and Bastogne, the 77th Fusilier Regiment on his left would attack Champs and Hemroulle. Most of the 26th Division artillery would support the attack from Flamierge and Givry and the 26th Reconnaissance Battalion would create a diversion to the south-west by attacking Isle de la Hesse. The rest of Kokott's available troops were not only exhausted, but in the case of the 901st Panzer Grenadiers and the 39th Grenadiers, had had to send companies south to help the 5th Parachute Division hold off the American 4th Armored Division. Oberst Maucke's battlegroup only reached Flamierge late on Christmas Eve and he protested to Gen Kokott, that he had been given no time for proper reconnaissance or the issue of orders. He was told to attack at 4am on Christmas Day.

That Christmas Eve Gen McAuliffe sent out a Christmas message to all his troops and his staff issued a Christmas card in the form of an outline map, with the words 'Merry Christmas' in green lettering at the centre and the enemy positions entirely surrounding Bastogne in red. It was much appreciated. During the

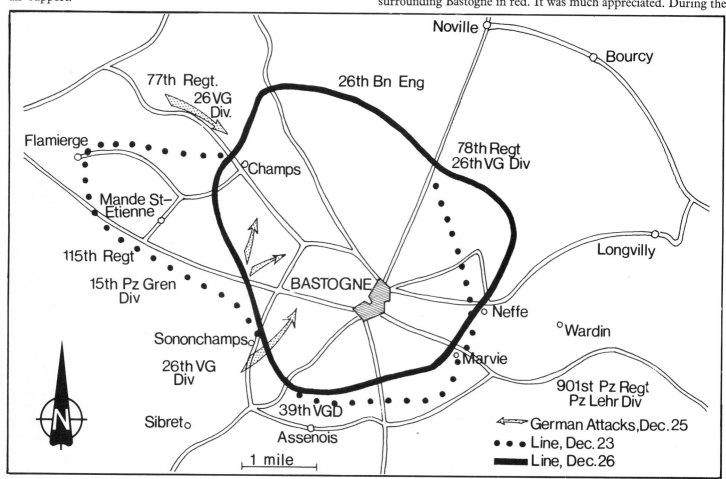

Above: Christmas Eve service in Bastogne./*US Army*

Right: Brig-Gen McAuliffe and his staff at Christmas dinner in Bastogne. McAuliffe is fourth from the left and Harry Kinnard second from the right./*US Army*

night the Luftwaffe bombed the town. hitting the aid post of the 20th Armored Infantry and burying 20 patients. The Hotel Lebrun, command post of the 10th Armored Division, was also hit and their Christmas Tree knocked over. The doll from its top was damaged in the fall and was ceremoniously awarded the Purple Heart. At Rolle, north-west of Bastogne, Col Steve Chappuis and most of his 502nd regimental staff went to midnight mass in the chapel of the Chateau, a service attended by many of the villagers – but they were to have a short night. Less than two hours after the service, at 2.45 on Christmas morning, the whole of the 502nd's front came under heavy shelling. At 3.30 Capt Wallace Swanson from Company A in their slit trenches north of Champs, reported enemy infantry on top of them and a few minutes later the telephone lines went dead. This was an attack by two battalions of the 77th Fusilier Regiment. Lt-Col Patrick Cassidy, the regimental executive, woke his colonel, Steve Chappuis, at Rolle Chateau and the whole of the 1st Battalion stood to arms. Company B moved forward to help Company A in Champs, where hand to hand fighting was now raging, one platoon going to the woods north-east of Champs to ensure contact, with the 2nd Battalion 502nd on the right of the 1st Battalion. At the same time Rolle itself came under heavy mortar and shell fire, their landlines to division were cut and radio communication failed too.

As the light improved, the 1st Battalion's intelligence officer Lt Samuel Nickels ran into the regimental command post, shouting 'Seven enemy tanks and lots of infantry are coming over the hill to your left.' In minutes the Chateau emptied as clerks, signallers and cooks snatched up their weapons and, led by Capt James Stone, ran to take up firing positions facing west. Company C and part of Company B also faced westwards and in the regimental aid post the surgeon, Maj Douglas Davidson, turned out the walking wounded to help with the defence.

Two hours before, at about 5am, Company A of the 327th Glider Infantry had reported 18 enemy tanks east of Mande Ste Etienne. By 7.10 these tanks and infantry from Oberst Maucke's 115th

UNATTENDED VEHICLES WILL BE IMPOUNDED BY MILITARY POLICE

Panzer Grenadier battlegroup, had broken right through the 3rd Battalion 327th's forward companies, whose colonel, Ray Allen, reported by radio to Col Harper that German tanks were within a hundred yards of his command post. Capt Thomas Reston from the reserve Company C, had telephoned to Allen 'Tanks are coming towards you. If you look out of your window now, you'll be looking right down the muzzle of an 88'. Ray Allen and two of his men ran from the command post to the woods, chased by tank fire all the way, and finally reached the lines of the 463rd Parachute Field Artillery in spite of some trigger-happy fire from his own side. From this artillery command post he was able to resume control of his companies by radio.

His glider infantry platoons had stayed in their trenches, letting the German tanks roll past them, and than popping up to engage the German infantry, capturing 92 of them. They counted 18 German tanks, all painted white, which now divided into two groups, one moving towards Hemroulle and the other driving north towards Rolle.

Two of the 705th's tank destroyers, positioned with the forward companies of the 3rd/327th had been knocked out, but not before they had destroyed two German tanks. Two more tank destroyers in Champs helped the 502nd's Company A by blowing apart houses held by the German infantry and another two were in position with the 502nd's Company C in the woods north of Hemroulle. The southernmost group of German tanks, coming from the west, now drew near to Company C's position, firing as they came and with infantry riding on the backs of the tanks. The American parachute troops fell back into the cover of the trees and there opened fire, knocking the German infantry off the tanks and as they did so, the German tanks swung left towards Champs, exposing their flanks at a range of about four hundred yards. Now the American tank destroyers opened fire and knocked out three

Mark IVs. Another was hit and stopped by a bazooka from Company C and a fifth by Capt Stone's scratch force from regimental headquarters. The German infantry were cut to pieces. Thirty of them were taken prisoner and 67 were left lying dead in front of the Company C wood. A lone Mark IV tank rattled on bravely into Champs, where it was finally burned up by hits from a bazooka and a six-pounder gun. Another Mark IV got right into Hemroulle and was there captured intact.

By 8am radio communication with division had been restored and Team Cherry, part of the Combat Command B, 10th Armored Division reserve, came out from Bastogne to reinforce the 502nd and the 327th, but the situation was already well in hand. The German 77th Fusiliers' attack on Champs had been beaten back with the loss of 98 men killed in the village and 81 captured. Not a single tank or soldier got back to the German lines from the 115th Panzer Grenadier group, to tell what had happened to their attack. All 18 tanks and most of two infantry battalions had been destroyed, killed or captured by the bazookas, machine guns and rifles of the 327th and the 502nd and the guns of the 705th Tank Destroyers and the 463rd Parachute Field Artillery.

Next day, 26 December, the leading tanks of the United States 4th Armored Division broke through the German 5th Parachute Division at Assenois and made contact with the 326th Airborne Engineers. At 5.10pm Lt-Col Creighton Abrams, commanding the leading tank battalion reported to Gen McAuliffe and the first convoy of 40 trucks and 70 ambulances moved into Bastogne that night. Much hard fighting still lay ahead, but the siege of Bastogne was over.

Above: A post from the 502nd Parachute Infantry north of Bastogne, turns back some Belgian civilians./*US Army*

Left: Olin Daws' picture of men of the 327th Glider Infantry, lining up for 'chow' in Hemroulle./*US War Dept*

Above left: German Mark IV tank knocked out in the fight for Champs./*US Army*

Left: Damaged Sherman tanks being recovered for repair, near Bastogne on 4 January. /*US Army*

Above: A Graves Registration Company collect Allied and enemy dead./*US Army*

Centre right: The US Military Cemetery at Foy in 1946. 2,700 Americans lie here, mostly from the garrison of Bastogne./*US Army*

Below right: The 101st Airborne Division memorial at Bastogne under construction in November 1949./*US Army*

12 The US Third Army Attack from the South

At Gen Eisenhower's conference in Verdun on 19 December Gen Patton received his orders to drive north into the left flank of the German advance, but with his customary, swift reaction, he had already made a number of preliminary moves. III Corps headquarters had been ordered up from Metz to north of Luxembourg; the 80th Infantry Division moved to Luxembourg and the 4th Armored to Longwy; and both III and XII Corps were warned to be ready for a move northwards. Gen Eddy at XII Corps now received orders to attack north-east to restore the southern shoulder of the German salient. Included in his Corps were the 4th Infantry Division; the 10th Armored Division, less Combat Command B in Bastogne; Combat Command A of the 9th Armored Division; the 109th Infantry of the 28th Division, which had fallen back to the south in the face of the massive assault by the German Fifth Panzer Army; and a fresh division from the south, the 5th Infantry.

On the left of XII Corps, Gen Millikin's III Corps were to strike due north to relieve Bastogne. The corps plan was for an advance with all three divisions in line, 4th Armored on the left, 26th Infantry in the centre and 80th Infantry on the right in contact

with XII Corps. Eleven field artillery battalions were added to III Corps for the advance and to each infantry division was allotted a tank and a tank destroyer battalion. Gen Patton told Gen Millikin 'Attack in column of regiments and drive like hell.' H-Hour was to be 6am on 22 December and their optimistic objective was St Vith.

The 80th Division moved off with the 319th Infantry on the left and the 318th on the right, crossing their start-line, the Mesch –

Below left: Lt-Gen George Patton, commanding the US Third Army. /*US Army*

Below: Signalmen of the 4th Armored Division laying telephone lines – Cpl Fisher tying in at the fence post and Pvts Busch and Aho on the truck./*US Army*

Right: Maj-Gen John Millikin, who commanded the US III Corps. /*US Army*

Below right: A German regular sailor who had served since 1938, captured by the US 26th Division, while fighting as an infantry soldier. /*US Army*

Arlon road at H-Hour. They reached Vichten, still held by the US 109th Infantry, and advanced to Merzig, where they bumped into the German 352nd Volksgrenadier Division, part of the Seventh Army marching westwards across their front. The Americans crashed into the German division's artillery, split the German force down the middle, and by nightfall had reached Heiderscheid and Ettelbruck. Here German resistance stiffened and both American regiments were held up. The reserve regiment, the 317th, was put in to attack Welscheid, but were beaten back with many casualties. On 24 December two battalions were taken from the 318th Infantry to reinforce the 4th Armored in their drive for Bastogne and from Christmas Day to 27 December the 319th Infantry continued their advance to Tadler on the River Sure. In these five days the 80th Division had inflicted serious damage on two German divisions and had delayed the move forward of German reinforcements, in particular the Führer Grenadier Brigade. All this helped considerably to weaken the German westward thrust and to ease the 4th Armored Division's task of breaking through to Bastogne.

On the left of the 80th Division, the 26th advanced with the 104th Infantry on the right and the 328th on the left. At Grosbous the 104th met the 915th Grenadier Regiment of the German 352nd Division and, joined by the survivors of the US 109th Infantry, eventually drove the Germans out of the village. On the west flank the 328th Infantry advanced six miles to Arsdorf and Rambrouch, but were here held up by a new German formation, the Führer Grenadier Brigade. This was a picked Army unit, made up of a tank battalion of Mark IV and V tanks, a battalion of panzer grenadiers in half-tracks and an infantry battalion on foot. Progress now slowed down. The 26th Division was new to battle and the infantry were reluctant to fight their way forward, preferring to follow the tanks and tank destroyers and relying heavily on fire support from artillery and the Quad .50s of their anti-aircraft battalion.

On the western flank of this III Corps advance, the 4th Armored Division had the vital job of breaking through the ring of German troops round Bastogne. This was Gen Patton's favourite division. They had made a great reputation for dash and drive in Normandy and during Patton's rapid advance across France, but by now much of their equipment was showing signs of wear, they were short of tanks and many of their men were inexperienced reinforcements. Their general, Hugh Gaffey, was a newcomer and so was Brig-Gen Herbert Earnest, leading Combat Command A. Gen Patton now ordered Gaffey to lead with his armour, engineers and artillery and to hold his infantry back, ready to clear enemy positions by-passed by the tanks. At 6am on 22 December they crossed their start-line from Habay-la-Neuve to Niedercolpach with Combat Command A moving up the main Arlon to Bastogne road and Combat Command B on secondary roads to the west. On the main road some delay was caused by the demolition made by the US VIII Corps engineers in their earlier creation of barrier lines to the Germans moving south, but the first contact with the Germans was at Martelange, where a rifle company of the German 15th Parachute Regiment held up the advance until early on 23 December. The broken bridge here was repaired by 3pm and Gen Millikin radioed Gen Middleton at VIII Corps in Neufchateau, that contact with the 101st Airborne Division in Bastogne was expected 'that night'. On the west Combat Command B had moved rapidly and by midday on 22 December, the first day of their advance, they had reached Burnon, only seven, miles from Bastogne. Here, however, they were held up by more demolitions, covered by fire from men of the 5th Parachute Division and the village was only cleared at midnight.

A few hours later anti-tank gun and machine gun fire from Chaumont showed that the place was strongly held. The American 10th Armored Infantry and 22 Shermans of the 8th Tank Battalion moved round to west and north of the village in the morning, while the artillery shelled it and fighter-bombers of the XIX Tactical Air Command attacked it from the air after a spectacular dog-fight high above Chaumont with Bf109s of the Luftwaffe.

At 1.30pm the American assault went in, with infantry riding on

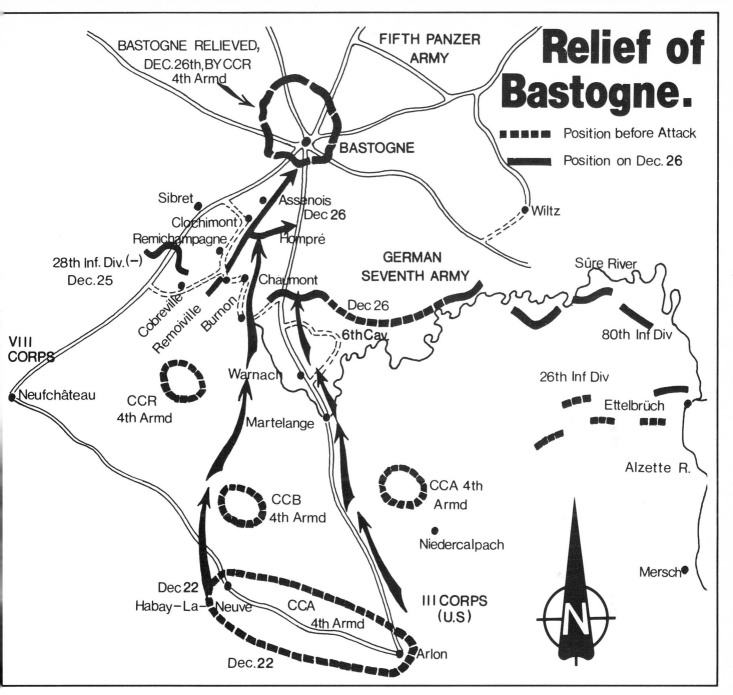

Relief of Bastogne.

▪▪▪▪▪ Position before Attack

━━━━ Position on Dec. 26

BASTOGNE RELIEVED, DEC. 26th, BY CCR 4th Armd

FIFTH PANZER ARMY

BASTOGNE

Sibret

Clochimont

Remichampagne

Assenois Dec 26

Pompré

Wiltz

28th Inf. Div. (-) Dec. 25

Chaumont

GERMAN SEVENTH ARMY

Sûre River

Cobreville

Remoiville

Burnon

Dec 26

6th Cav.

80th Inf Div

VIII CORPS

Warnach

26th Inf Div

Ettelbrüch

Neufchâteau

CCR 4th Armd

Martelange

CCA 4th Armd

Alzette R.

CCB 4th Armd

Niedercalpach

Mersch

Dec 22

Habay-La-Neuve

CCA 4th Armd

III CORPS (U.S)

Dec. 22

Arlon

N

Top left: Part of the cost of taking Chaumont. Two men of the 25th Cavalry lie dead, near their shattered jeep while *Left:* another jeep of their unit passes by, continuing the advance./*Both US Army*

the leading tanks, close behind the fighter-bomber and artillery barrage and more infantry moving in on foot. The afternoon sun had thawed the fields, so that some of the tanks bogged down, but the Americans captured the village and rounded up a company of the German 14th Parachute Regiment. Almost at once a counter-attack developed. Gen Kokott sent in the 11th Assault Gun Brigade, 10 to 15 Mark IV tank chassis, mounting 75mm guns, and carrying infantry from his 39th Grenadier Regiment. They rolled out of the woods north of Chaumont down the hill into the village and as their infantry jumped off and ran forward, the assault guns blasted the American tanks and the houses held by the 10th Armored Infantry. The American forward artillery observer was dead and they could not get their guns to fire, 11 Shermans were knocked out, the 10th Armored Infantry lost 65 men and their only officer left

alive, Lt Charles Guiot stayed to cover the withdrawal, until he too was killed. By dusk Combat Command B was back where they had started and Chaumont was once more in German hands.

On the same day, 23 December, Lt-Col Delk Oden's 35th Tank Battalion and Company G 51st Armored Infantry attacked War-nach. In the village were the German 15th Parachute Regiment headquarters and a parachute battalion, supported by a battery of assault guns. The first American attacks during the night were beaten back, but the next day the American tanks and infantry went in again from three sides of the village and a furious house to house battle followed. Both sides fought desperately. Four Sher-mans were destroyed and as each house was cleared, the German parachute infantry counter-attacked in savage rushes. The Ameri-cans pressed forward slowly but relentlessly, until finally the village was won. 135 German dead were counted and a similar number taken prisoner at a cost to the Americans of 68 men killed and wounded.

A few miles to the east, in the gap developing between the US 4th Armored and 26th Infantry Divisions, German tanks and infantry had appeared and seemed to threaten the 4th Armored's right flank. Gen Gaffey therefore sent his Combat Command Reserve to capture Bigonville to protect his right. Col Wendell

Blanchard with the 37th Tank Battalion and the 53rd Armored Infantry were held up by fire from the woods south of the village, but early on 24 December they attacked with two infantry/tank teams after a sharp concentration of fire from their artillery. More house to house fighting ended in the encirclement of the village by the Americans and the capture of 328 men from the German 13th Parachute Regiment.

At Chaumont, Warnach and Bigonville, Oberst Heilbron's 5th Parachute Division had lost heavily, but the Americans were now short of tanks and their attempts to 'bounce' a way through by armour only had failed. Gen Millikin now ordered his three divisions to spend the rest of 24 December resting and building up their strength for a major effort on Christmas Day. The 1st Bat-

talion 318th Infantry were moved across from the 80th Division to bolster the infantry strength of Combat Command A and the 2nd Battalion joined Combat Command B. Both these battalions were short of men and the 1st Battalion's casualties had been such, that the commanding officer and all the company commanders were new to their commands. In Bastogne hopes had been raised for an earlier relief and in the evening of 23 December McAuliffe sent a message to Gaffey 'Sorry I did not get to shake hands today. I was disappointed' and a later message from his staff to the 4th Armored read 'There is only one more shopping day to Christmas'.

On Christmas Day the advance began again. Late in the night before Combat Command Reserve had moved across form Bigonville on the division's right flank to Neufchateau on the left with

Above: Pvt Kelly, a military policeman of the 4th Armored Division, escorts a group of prisoners to the rear, as a half-track goes by them./*US Army*

Left: A 4th Armored light tank brings in two wounded men to an aid post./*US Army*

Right: The grave of a German soldier from 5th Parachute Division near Warnach. /*US Army*

Far right: Sgt Hobart Drew, a tank crewman of 37th Tank Battalion, wounded twice in these battles./*US Army*

orders to drive up the Neufchateau-Bastogne road. They reached their assembly area at Berdreux before dawn on Christmas Day. In Combat Command A Maj George Connaughton led his 1st Battalion 318th into action for his first time in an attack on Tintange, helped by No 377 Fighter Squadron's bombs and rockets, and captured the village after a bitter and costly fight. The 51st Armored Infantry reached Hollange, while the 2nd Battalion 318th Infantry with Combat Command B retook Chaumont and the woods round it, slowly and methodically clearing the German paratroopers from their foxholes. In this second fight for Chaumont Sgt Paul Wiedorfer of the 2nd Battalion 118th Infantry won the Medal of Honor. Although wounded, he rushed a house held by the Germans, killing, wounding and capturing all the 40 men in it.

On the left Combat Command Reserve started north as a combined team of Lt-Col Creighton Abram's 37th Tank Battalion and Lt-Col George Jacques 53rd Armored Infantry, supported by the 94th Armored Field Artillery and a battery of Long Tom 155mm guns of the 177th Field Artillery.

Remonville was heavily shelled by four battalions of artillery and as the American tanks and infantry rode into the village amongst the last of their own shells, the Germans of the 3rd Battalion, 14th Parachute Regiment ran out to meet them, too late to reach their fire positions. Tank machine gunners and American riflemen cut them down, grenades into windows and cellars dug out the survivors and by evening the battle was over and 327 prisoners had been taken.

During the next day, 26 December, the American fighter-bombers and artillery hammered the German 5th Parachute Division, whose own artillery were now running out of ammunition. Some of their men began to give up more easily, but others held out at crossroads, in farms and among the woods, inflicting casualties on the advancing Americans and slowing down their advance. By dark the 2nd Battalion 318th Infantry had reached Hompré, 4,000 yards from the Bastogne perimeter defences and at 4.30am on 27 December Lt Walter Carr led a patrol into Bastogne and returned with a map, showing the positions of the 101st Airborne Division. But other Americans had got there first.

Early on Boxing Day morning Combat Command Reserve started out over the frozen ground towards Remichampagne. P-47 fighter-bombers from the 362nd Fighter Group came over and, bombing close ahead of the tanks, eased the way forward through the woods and villages. As they drew near to Clochimont, where they expected to meet the main line of German resistance, the tanks deployed each side of the village. Their plan called for a continued advance up the main road to Bastogne through Sibret, but the latter was known to be strongly held by the German 26th Reconnaissance Battalion. Abrams and Jacques stood in the road, discussing the situation and watching the C-47s dropping supplies over Bastogne. Then Abrams suggested a dash for Bastogne straight up the side road through Assenois. Jacques agreed and Abrams called over the air for his battalion operations officer, Captain William Dwight, to bring Team C forward. This consisted of Company C of the tanks and Company C of the infantry. Three battalions of artillery, borrowed from Combat Command B and their own 94th Armored Artillery were registered and ready to fire on Assenois and Abrams told Dwight to take Team C into Assenois and on to Bastogne.

At 4.20pm they set off, the Shermans leading and the infantry half-tracks close behind them. Four minutes later Lieutenant Charles Boggess in the leading tank called for fire and 13 batteries fired 10 rounds at intense rates into the village. Boggess called again for the fire to lift and drove into the village, now darkened by the dense smoke and dust of the gunfire. American medium artillery shells were still crashing down, as the thin-skinned half-tracks arrived and the infantry jumped out of them to find cover in the houses. The German garrison from both the 5th Parachute and 26th Divisions fought hard and it was all Company C of the 53rd Armored Infantry could do to hold them. Five tanks and one half-track, led by Boggess, drove through the village, but the German infantry threw out some Teller mines into the 300 yard gap between the three leading tanks and the half-track. The half-track blew up on the first mine. Capt Dwight ran the two following tanks onto the road verge and jumped out with his crew to lift the mines. Then they roared on after the others. At 4.50pm Boggess spotted some Americans on the road ahead and on coming up to them, found they were men of the 326th Airborne Engineers. Contact with the Bastogne garrison had been made.

Twenty minutes later Lt-Col Abrams reported to Gen McAuliffe, who had come forward to the engineers' outpost line and the two men shook hands. Back in Assenois Jacques' 53rd Infantry were still fighting to clear the village. S/Sgt James Hendrix won the Medal of Honor for his single-handed attack on two 88mm guns and the woods north of the village were swept by Company A, directed by Capt Frank Kutak from a jeep, as he had been wounded in both legs. By 1am the area was clear enough for the road to be opened and the light tank company of the 37th escorted into Bastogne 40 trucks, full of ammunition and stores and 70 ambulances.

Above: A patrol of the 511st Armored
Infantry near Bastogne./*US Army*

Right: Receipt for the town of Bastogne,
signed by the VIII Corps Commander,
Maj-Gen Troy Middleton./*US Army*

MEMORANDUM RECEIPT
VIII CORPS

DATE 18 JAN 1945

RECEIVED FROM THE 101ST AIRBORNE DIVISION

THE TOWN OF BASTOGNE, LUXEMBOURG PROVINCE, BELGIUM

CONDITION: USED BUT SERVICEABLE, KRAUT DISINFECTED

SIGNED

TROY H. MIDDLETON
MAJ GENERAL USA
COMMANDING

13 The Germans Drive for the Meuse

While the 26th Volksgrenadier and Panzer Lehr Divisions were fighting to capture Bastogne, Oberst von Lauchert's Panzer Division was ordered to press on towards the Meuse. Early on 22 December they were over the River Ourthe at Ortheuville and waiting for petrol. Moving again on the 23rd they were held up for some time by demolition at the cross-roads west of Champlon, touched off by the US 51st Engineers, but the leading battalion of the 304th Panzer Grenadiers overran the US 4th Cavalry Group

at Harsin and reached Hargimont in the dark. This was the first contact with troops of the US 3rd Armored Division, hurrying down from the north to extend the right flank of the US XVIII Airborne Corps. That evening Gen von Lüttwitz came forward to urge on his armour, relieved the 304th's colonel of his command on the grounds that he lacked drive, sent him to the rear for court-martial and drove his troops on through the night as far as Buissonville.

On the right of this advance by the 2nd Panzer Division was the 116th Panzer Division. After breaking through the US 28th Infantry Division in the first two days of the battle, the 116th had found Houffalize undefended and the reconnaissance battalion had pressed on to Bertogne, and Salle to the south-west, looking for crossings over the River Ourthe. The stout-hearted defence of these crossings and the blowing of the bridges by small American engineer and tank destroyer detachments convinced Walther Krüger the commander of the German LVIII Corps, that there was no quick way through there and he ordered the 116th Panzers to turn about, cross the Ourthe at Houffalize and move north-westwards. This meant turning round a complete armoured division on one

Left: German transport crosses a partially destroyed bridge, built by US engineers. A 20mm anti-aircraft gun stands by./*IWM*

Below: Houffalize, drawn by Harrison Standley. The 116th Panzer Division went through here unopposed on 18 December./*US War Dept*

Above left: Tanks of the 3rd Armored Division moving towards Samree./*IWM*

Centre left: Americans examining smashed German armour on the road to Samree./*IWM*

Right: Pvt Forrester watches from the turret of a Sherman in Hotton, while Sgt Stozer mans a Browning machine gun./*US Army*

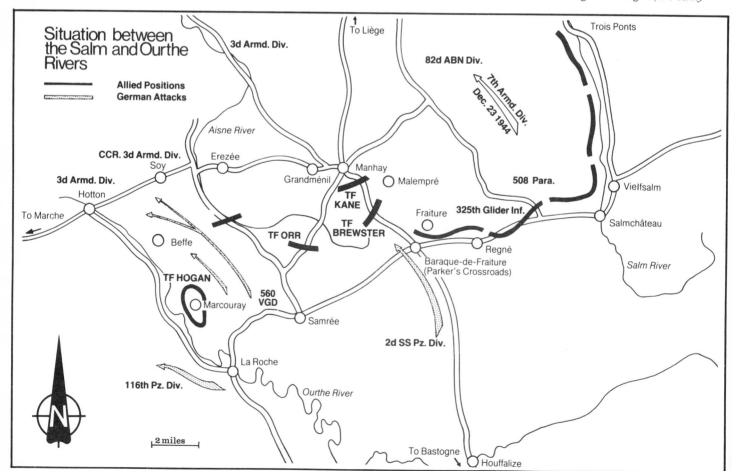

Situation between the Salm and Ourthe Rivers

▬▬▬▬ Allied Positions
▬▬▬▬ German Attacks

To Liège

Trois Ponts

3d Armd. Div.

82d ABN Div.

7th Armd. Div.
Dec. 23 1944

Aisne River

CCR. 3d Armd. Div.

Soy

Erezée

Grandménil

Manhay

Malempré

508 Para.

Vielfsalm

3d Armd. Div.

Hotton

TF KANE

Fraiture

325th Glider Inf.

Salmchâteau

To Marche

Beffe

TF ORR

TF BREWSTER

Regné

Salm River

TF HOGAN

Baraque-de-Fraiture
(Parker's Crossroads)

560 VGD

Marcouray

Samrée

2d SS Pz. Div.

La Roche

116th Pz. Div.

Ourthe River

N

2 miles

To Bastogne

Houffalize

road in the dark and led to considerable delay and a lot of cursing. It also, as it turned out, deflected the 116th from its thrust straight westwards, where there were very few American troops, to a more northerly advance, where the American 82nd Airborne and 3rd Armored Divisions were moving rapidly into position. The 116th Panzer Division commander, Gen von Waldenburg, later described it as a decision 'fatal to his division'.

By this time, 20 December, the other division of LVIII Corps, the 560th Volksgrenadier, had caught up on foot, a 'fine march performance' and by noon that day both divisions were north of the River Ourthe and moving towards Samrée and Rochefort. In both these towns were the supply columns of the US 7th Armored Division, who were still fighting near St Vith, far to the east. The divisional quartermaster, Lt-Col Miller, organised the best defence he could, but the German 60th Panzer Grenadier and 16th Panzer Regiment were not to be denied and chased out most of the American trucks. Task Force Tucker, part of the 3rd Armored Division's Combat Command A, tried to counter-attack, but lost six Shermans and from La Roche Lt Averill led two Shermans and a tank destroyer to join the fight at Samrée. They were not seen again.

These American administrative units had fought well and delayed the 116th Panzer considerably. Yet the Germans had captured in Samrée 25,000gal of petrol and 15,000 rations, enabling them to refuel all their tanks and vehicles. General Krüger still believed, that there was little organised American resistance in front of his corps and the Bayer battlegroup from the 116th hurried on to Hotton. Here was a two-way, Class 70 wooden bridge over the River Ourthe and on this morning of 21 December the village was held by 200 men from service detachments of the 3rd Armored Division and a platoon of the 51st Engineers, led by Capt Preston Hodges. With them were two medium tanks and a light tank, two 40mm Bofors guns and a 37mm anti-tank gun. A mile to the south in the village of Hampteau was an American engineer squad of 12 men.

Early in the morning the German tanks and infantry attacked out of the woods to the east, under cover of mortar fire. The Americans blocked the road into the village with trucks, but the leading

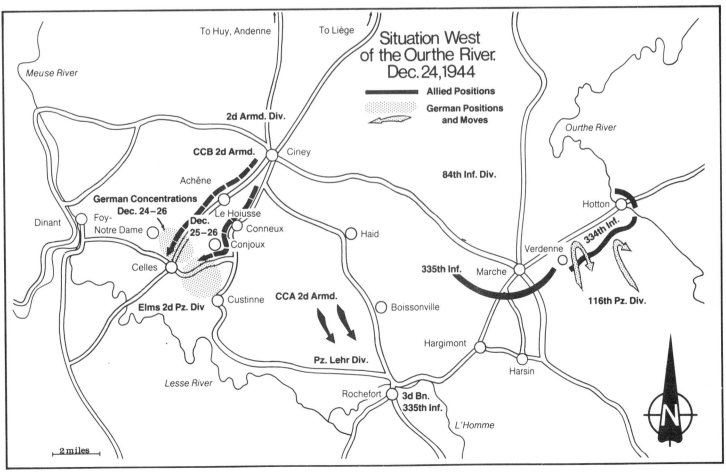

Left: A German soldier, killed in the house to house fighting in Hotton on 21 December. /*US Army*

Below: Self-propelled 105mm howitzers of the 3rd Armored Division in action./*US Army*

Bottom: Two German tanks knocked out in the fight for Hotton./*US Army*

Right: Pvt Melvin Biddle of the 517th Parachute Infantry./*US Army*

Bottom right: The 2nd Battalion 32nd Tank Regiment using its Shermans to fire indirect at enemy targets over the hill./*US Army*

German tanks were able to knock out both American tanks and to shoot at their infantry in the houses on the east bank of the river. At this point an American tank destroyer appeared and destroyed a Panther tank and the Americans in the village poured a hail of machine gun and rifle fire into the German positions. Most of the American trucks and ambulances were got away safely to the north and two more German tanks were destroyed by bazookas. At about 2 pm Combat Command Reserve from the 3rd Armored Division came in from Soy and Col Howze's attack drew the German tanks out of the town. At the same time Howze slipped some tanks and infantry into Hotton from the north and later in the afternoon two platoons reached Hotton from the American 84th Infantry Division. On the next day, 22 December, Col Howze launched a night attack along the Soy – Hotton road against a battlegroup of the 116th Panzer Division, using the newly arrived 1st Battalion, 517th Parachute Infantry, who had been sent to join the 3rd Armored Division to give them more infantry. Together with some tank destroyers they were thrown into the attack in the dark over unreconnoitred ground only half an hour after leaving their trucks and were eventually driven back after some bitter fighting. Pvt Melvin Biddle, a battalion scout, guided the battalion for much of the way and killed 17 Germans with 19 shots from his rifle. He was later awarded the Medal of Honor.

Gen Krüger was convinced by this defence of Hotton, that here too was no easy way through to the Meuse. He ordered the 116th to pull back to La Roche, cross the Ourthe there and move on to Marche. The 560th Volksgrenadier Division were to continue the attack towards Hotton and now in the evening of 21 December, the 2nd SS Panzer Division were coming up to join the right flank of Gen Krüger's LVIII Corps.

While the battle for Hotton was raging, Task Force Orr, part of the 3rd Armored Division's Combat Command Reserve, were having a brisk firefight with the 108th Grenadier Regiment from the 560th Division, at Dochamps. Losing three tanks, Orr finally withdrew to Amonines. Another Task Force, led by Lt-Col Hogan, was cut off at Marcouray, south of La Roche, by the 116th Panzer Division. Short of petrol, he was unable to break out to the north and although located by the Germans, he was not seriously attacked. On 23 December German officers appeared with a white flag, demanding his surrender and were told to come and get Marcouray, if they wanted it. An infantry attack that afternoon was beaten back and an American attempt to fire medical supplies into his position in leaflet shells only succeeded in damaging the stores irreparably. A supply drop by air went astray and Hogan eventually destroyed his tanks and vehicles and led his men back to the American lines on foot.

By the night of 22 and 23 December the German LVIII Panzer Korps was ready to attack north-westwards, with the 116th Panzer Division on the left, across the River Ourthe at La Roche and preparing to move on Marche; with the 560th Volksgrenadiers in the centre fighting for the Erezée–Soy–Hotton road; and coming up on the right the 2nd SS Panzer Division, directed on Manhay. This was a major threat to the US XVIII Airborne Corps, stretched out from Trois Ponts on the Salm River in the east to Hotton in the west, a 25-mile front thinly held by the 82nd Airborne and the 3rd Armored Divisions. On the eastern flank the 505th and 508th Parachute Regiments had held up the remnants of the German 1st SS Panzer Division and were now to come under increasing pressure from the 9th SS Panzer Division, at last able to reach the front through the traffic jams in the German rear areas. The 325th Glider Infantry filled the wide gap between Salmchateau and Fraiture, backed up by what battered remnants of the 7th Armored

Left: Lt-Col Hogan's men reach the American lines near Hotton – their faces camouflaged, glad of a meal, but still carrying their personal weapons./*US Army*

Bottom: La Roche./*IWM*

Right: Men of the 2nd Battalion 325th Glider Infantry march towards Fraiture./*US Army*

Centre right: Maj-Gen Maurice Rose, commanding the 3rd Armored Division at a medal presentation in October 1944./*US Army*

Bottom right: A parachute soldier from the 82nd Airborne Division goes out on a reconnaissance, covered by his fox-hole companion./*US Army*

and 106th Infantry Divisions had escaped from the St Vith cauldron. Here, in the centre of the XVIII Airborne Corps line and at the junction of the 82nd and 3rd Divisions was the vital crossroads at Baraque de Fraiture on the main road from Bastogne through Houffalize to Manhay and Liège and coming up it was the full strength of the fresh 2nd SS Panzer Division.

Three days before, late on 19 December, the first American troops to reach these crossroads were three 105mm howitzers from the 589th Field Artillery Battalion, led by Maj Arthur Parker. Part of the 106th Division, they were all that remained of his regiment, wiped out on the Schnee Eifel with the 422nd and 423rd Infantry. Next day four half-tracks arrived, mountin Quad .50 machine guns from the 203rd Anti-Aircraft Artillery Battalion. On 21 December in the early morning darkness a German patrol of 80 men marched up the road from the south and were cut to pieces by the Quad .50s. They were men of the 560th Volksgrenadier division and with the prisoners was an officer from the 2nd SS Panzers, reconnoitring a route forward for his division. That afternoon D Troop, 87th Cavalry Squadron, joined the defence, sent there by Gen Hasbrouck from his 7th Armored Division and during that night 11 Sherman tanks from the 3rd Armored Division's Task Force Kane pulled in. Gen Gavin from the 82nd and Gen Rose of 3rd Armored discussed together how best to hold this area and before dawn on 22 December the 2nd Battalion, 325th Glider Infantry marched into Fraiture village, sending on Company F under Capt Junior Woodruff to the crossroads. However this reinforcement was counter-balanced by the departure of Kane's tanks at noon on 22 December to join the battle round Dochamps and Samrée.

Above: 3rd Armored Division tanks near Manhay, held up by a blockage ahead, watch the woods alongside the road./*US Army*

Left: Pvt Vernon Haught returns from three hours on out-post duty for a hot meal and some sleep./*US Army*

Above right: Temporary shelters, dug into a hillside by men of the 82nd Airborne Division./*US Army*

Right: Harrison Standley's drawing of La Roche./*US War Dept*

During this same day, 22 December, the 2nd SS Panzer Division was halted in its assembly areas nine miles south of the Baraque de Fraiture crossroads, waiting for fuel. By nightfall enough had arrived to allow the 4th Panzer Grenadier Regiment to advance with some tanks and guns and they relieved the men of the 560th Division, watching the crossroads. Patrols moved right round the crossroads to the north, cutting the road to Manhay and capturing in the early morning four American tank destroyers from the 643rd Battalion, as they drove south to reinforce the crossroads garrison.

Early on 23 December the 2nd Battalion of the 4th Panzer Grenadiers, moving through the woods on the right of the main road, made a surprise attack on the village of Fraiture. After some bitter hand to hand fighting they were driven back by the American glider troops. The 4th Panzer Grenadiers' 3rd Battalion had meanwhile followed their patrols round to the north of the crossroads, but three Sherman tanks got through them to the crossroads in time to join the battle. This began at 4pm with a heavy shelling of the American positions, clearly visible in the small snow-covered area held by the defence.

Captured American radios were used by the Germans to jam the American artillery nets and two panzer companies rolled forward in the final assault, together with the whole infantry strength of two panzer grenadier battalions. At 5pm Captain Woodruff asked for permission to withdraw, but was told to hold on at all costs. It was soon over. Two German tanks had been destroyed and three

American tanks had got away by the time that Col Charles Billingslea of the 325th finally gave the word to get out. Some men escaped, when a herd of cattle stampeded across the road, but only 44 out of Company F's 116 got back to their battalion in Fraiture.

By the evening of 23 December the German thrusts in the centre were still making progress, as the 2nd SS Panzers, fresh from their capture of the Baraque de Fraiture crossroads, threatened Manhay and the junction of the US 82nd Airborne and 3rd Armored Divisions. The 116th Panzer Division had crossed the river Ourthe at La Roche and were approaching Marche and Hotton, both now held by the newly arrived 334th Infantry of the 84th Infantry Division. To the south of this advance General von Lüttwitz's XLVII Panzer Corps were making for the Meuse with Von Lauchert's 2nd Panzer Division in the lead. Indeed by the evening

of 22 December his reconnaissance battalion had reached Celles, only four miles from the Meuse. Bayerlein's Panzer Lehr Division had been unable to clear Rochefort on 23 December, as the American 3rd Battalion 335th Infantry had got into the town the day before and were only driven out after a hard fight all day on Christmas Eve. Forty miles away to the north-east the 12th SS Panzer Division now finally gave up trying to break through the US V Corps after two days of bloody and bitter fighting for Butgenbach against the 26th Infantry. The US, 99th, 2nd and 1st Divisions had held firm on the northern shoulder throughout the battle and had so prevented Sepp Dietrich from widening the breach in the American lines made by the 1st SS Panzer Division. Only now, almost a week late, were his two reserve divisions, 2nd and 9th SS Panzer, able to get forward into action.

Above: A Sherman, well concealed by the roadside just south of Manhay. /*US Army*

Left: Capt Gray, a 'Phantom' patrol officer in his jeep with a radio operator and a driver-gunner./*IWM*

Another failure to break the American northern shoulder occurred at Malmedy on 21 December, where Skorzeny's 150th Panzer Brigade were beaten back with heavy losses by the 120th Infantry and in Stoumont and La Gleize Jochen Peiper's battle-group of the 1st SS Panzer Division had by now been trapped by the US 119th Infantry and the 3rd Armored Division's Combat Command B.

On the American side the main concern was the approach to the Meuse of the 2nd Panzer and Panzer Lehr Divisions and the threat to the north-west and the Allied extension of the northern shoulder, posed by the 2nd SS and 9th SS Panzer Divisions, backed up by the 560th Volksgrenadiers.

Gen Matthew Ridgway's XVIII Airborne Corps on 23 December were still holding a wide front in the form of a salient from Trois Ponts in the east, down to Vielsalm and then west to Fraiture – a distance of 16 miles. Extending the line westwards was the 3rd Armored Division and already moving into position on their right again at Hotton and Marche were the regiments of the 84th Infantry Division. Twelve miles north of Marche the US 2nd Armored Division were in reserve and nearby was the 74th Division, coming up to join Gen Lawton Collins's VII Corps.

It was on 23 December, too, that the battered and exhausted garrions of St Vith had pulled back through Vielsalm into the shelter of the 82nd Airborne's defence line. Field Marshal Montgomery had now been in command of the northern shoulder of the battle and of the US First Army, V, XVIII and VII Corps for four days. He had visited the army commander and all the corps commanders and his liaison officers had covered the whole front. British 'Phantom' patrols of an officer and six driver/operators from the GHQ Signal Regiment with a direct radio link to Headquarters 21st Army Group had been with V Corps since the first day, 16 December, in Bastogne and later Neufchateau with VIII Corps and with the XVIII Airborne and VII Corps since 18 December. Capt Hills with the 'Phantom' patrol at Gen Simpson's US Ninth

Army headquarters further north was told by an American major 'Well, we're all right now'. 'Are we?' said Hills and the American went on: 'Yes. Our Field Marshal and George Patton will do the job between them'.

Capt Borman at the US VIII Corps headquarters sat up with Gen Middleton through the anxious night of 18 December, as reports poured in of German penetration along the whole corps front and next morning drove out of the town with him 'as men of the 101st Airborne Division were moving in silently from the west on either side of us'. At Gen Ridgeway's XVIII Airborne Corps Capt the Honourable Michael Astor reported 'I have never seen a Corps headquarters occupying so little space' and he went on to remark on Matthew Ridgway's air of resolute confidence and his stern and unflinching attitude. Ridgway's approach to battle was now to have a severe test, as Monty decided to tidy up the battle-field still further and to strengthen the Allied line in the north by pulling back the 82nd Airborne from their Vielsalm salient to a shorter line through Bra to Manhay. It went against the grain for these parachute and glider troops to give up ground and both Gavin and Ridgway protested. However, the orders stood and the regiments of the 82nd pulled back to their new, shorter line under heavy pressure from the 2nd SS panzer Division and the Führer Begleit Brigade on the right and the newly arrived 9th SS Panzer Division on the left. The first troops into action from this division were the 19th Panzer Grenadier Regiment, who crossed the river at Vielsalm on Christmas Eve in face of spirited resistance by two platoons of the 508th Parachute Infantry. These panzer grenadiers were Germans, whose families had been settled for generations near the Black Sea and they were a fine fighting regiment. They followed up closely, as the 508th withdrew, and in the next three days attacked fiercely the American parachute troops in their new

positions at Erria and Villettes, driving them out of both villages. Supported by accurate artillery fire, the 3rd Battalion, 508th, led by their colonel, Louis Mendez, counter-attacked with equal ferocity next day, recaptured the village and restored the American defence line. Over 100 German dead were found in the villages and the 19th Panzer Grenadiers were reported to have been cut to pieces.

Next day the 2nd SS Panzer Division attacked Manhay and Ridgway was forced to throw into the battle the tired remnants of the 7th Armored and 106th Infantry Divisions to support the 3rd Armored. In a bitter struggle for the village 19 American tanks

were lost and 100 men killed and wounded. The SS tanks had an open road to the north and the rear areas of the US First Army, but their eyes were still fixed on the Meuse and in Manhay they turned left on the road to the west. But by now the next village, Soy, was firmly held by the US 75th Division and the 2nd SS Panzers were stopped dead in their tracks.

Gen Ridgway, furious at the loss of Manhay, ordered Gen Hasbrouck to retake the village at once and this the 7th Armored Division succeeded in doing by Boxing Day, helped by the 2nd Battalion, 424th Infantry, one of the few units left from the wreck of the 106th Division. On Christmas Eve the 116th Panzer Division were driven back from Marche and Hotton by the 334th Infantry and away to the west near Celles, British armoured cars from the Household Cavalry were in action with the leading units of the 2nd Panzer Division. In the American 2nd Armored Division Gen Harmon was told of this contact and at the same time two American P-51 fighters were shot at by light flak from Celles. This

confirmed his belief that there was a lot of German armour in that area and he ordered his Combat Command B to move forward to Ciney. At the same time he sent two of his artillery regiments into fire positions, ready to support the advance of Combat Command B. Then he radioed to VII Corps, asking urgently for permission to attack.

At Corps headquarters and also at First Army there was concern about the apparent threat from four German panzer divisions – 2nd, Panzer Lehr, 116th and 9th – and round Manhay the American 3rd and 7th Armored Divisions looked like being brushed aside by the 2nd SS Panzer. The VII Corps Commander, Gen Collins, was out touring his divisions and his chief of staff, Brig Willie Palmer, passed on to First Army Ernie Harmon's request. Maj-Gen Bill Kean, the First Army chief of staff, told Palmer 'roll with the punch, but use your discretion', meaning that the VII Corps should keep its defence line intact, even if it meant withdrawing. He also sent a liaison officer, Col Akers, to make sure the message was understood and on his arrival, Collins made Akers confirm the orders in writing.

To Collins, however, the situation looked less gloomy than it did to those at First Army. His left flank was now held firmly by the 84th and 75th Divisions and if the reports were true that the Germans were running short of petrol, this might be the moment for attack, not withdrawal. Akers went back to First Army at Tongres with Collins' views and Collins himself explained them by telephone to Kean and Gen Hodges, his Army Commander. That same evening he called Ernie Harmon and told him to attack next morning. Ernie Harmon shouted down the telephone 'the bastards are in the bag'.

On Christmas morning Brig-Gen Isaac White's Combat Command B set off from Ciney to the south-west to look for their

Above left: Pvt Harrison of the 643rd Tank Destroyer Battalion looks down at the body of an 82nd Airborne Division soldier, killed near Erria./*US Army*

Left: A 75mm pack howitzer of Battery B, 376th Parachute Field Artillery in action near Villettes./*US Army*

Far left: Maj-Gen Jim Gavin, commanding the 82nd Airborne Division visits the 508th at Erria./*US Army*

Above: An SS Soldier captured in Manhay on Boxing Day./*US Army*

Right: A Panther, knocked out near Manhay. /*IWM*

Below: Men of the 84th Division digging in near Amonines./*US Army*

namesakes, von Lauchert's 2nd Panzer Division. Lt-Col Harry Hillyard's Task Force A went through Achêne and Le Horisse, while Task Force B, led by Maj Clifton Batchelder, drove through Conneux and Conjoux. Above them the fighter-bombers of the American 37th Fighter Group and 83 Group RAF were up in swarms and lower down American L-19 light aircraft had a field day, picking up targets for both the artillery and the air strikes.

The leading battlegroup of the 2nd Panzers was by now split in two. The reconnaissance battalion and part of the artillery were at Foy Notre Dame, four miles from Dinant. Here they were attacked by the 82nd Reconnaissance Battalion of the 2nd Armored Division and the 3rd Royal Tank Regiment from the British 29th Armoured Brigade. The Germans lost seven Panther tanks, but made quite a fight of it, until they were finally overwhelmed, their commanding officer and 147 men being captured.

Maj Cochenhausen with a tank battalion, a regiment of panzer grenadiers and the rest of his artillery, handicapped now by a lack of fuel, took cover in the woods between Celles and Conjoux and here they were shelled and bombed by the 2nd Armored artillery, RAF Typhoons and American P-38 fighter-bombers. Finally both Task Force A and B closed in and drove through the woods on Boxing Day and the day after, killing or capturing the survivors of 2nd Panzer. Maj Cochenhausen and 600 of his men reached Rochefort on foot, where the rest of his division had rallied on Boxing Day, but the 2nd Panzer Division had suffered the crippling loss of all the reconnaissance battalion, the 304th Panzer Grenadier

Regiment, all the tanks and guns of the 3rd Panzer Regiment's 2nd Battalion and three battalions of artillery.

All through these three days von Lauchert had been well aware of the threat to his leading battlegroup and had asked in vain for permission to withdraw them in time. Two attempts by the Panzer Lehr Division to reach Celles were stopped on Christmas Day by Allied air attacks. In a further attempt to widen the narrow German thrust to the west, Panzer Lehr also attacked Humain, driving out the armoured cars and light tanks of Troop A 24th Cavalry Squadron. Col MacDonald's 4th Cavalry Group tried to retake it, but by this time the village had been strongly garrisoned by the 9th Panzer Division, veterans of Arnhem, and it was only on 27 December that the village was once more in the hands of the 2nd Armored Division.

On Boxing Day von Lauchert himself led a small battlegroup from Hargimont, where his troops had been relieved by the 9th Panzer Division, through Ciergnon, as far as Grande and Petite

Trisogne, almost into Celles, But from these two villages he saw the ridge ahead crawling with British and American tanks and at the same time his column was spotted by no less then five artillery observation aircraft. Almost at once intense artillery concentrations fell on his battlegroup, followed by a series of fighter-bomber attacks. Luckily for his column's survival a radio message came in from XLVII Panzer Corps just at this time, ordering both 2nd Panzer and Panzer Lehr to pull back to Rochefort.

On this same day, 26 December, Hitler at last recognised that his dream of reaching Antwerp and splitting the Allied armies was over. He gave in to the pleas of his commanders, authorised the

withdrawal of the Fifth Panzer Army spearheads and ordered the immediate capture of Bastogne. General Guderian, Chief of the Army General Staff, tried vainly to persuade Hitler that the Ardennes campaign should be stopped at once and the troops transferred to the Eastern Front. Like most German soldiers, he viewed with dread the massive Russian winter offensives which were about to begin and the threat to Prussia and all eastern Germany of invasion by their ancient enemies, the Slav hordes.

All available troops were now switched to Bastogne – the remnants of the 1st SS Panzer Division, 3rd Panzer Grenadier and 26th Volksgrenadier Divisions, the Führer Begleit and Führer Grenadier Brigades, the 115th Panzer Grenadier Regiment and a few days later, the 9th and 12th SS Panzer and 340th and 167th Volksgrenadier Divisions.

Much hard fighting lay ahead, but Boxing Day marked the end of the German offensive. Now it was the Allies' turn to attack, to eliminate the Bulge and to trap as many Germans as they could.

Below: An American 76mm anti-tank gun, knocked out in the fight for Humain./*US Army*

Bottom: Three of the tank wrecks, left behind in Humain by the 9th Panzer Division./*US Army*

14 The Allies Counter-Attack

Above: Gen Patton in Bastogne on 30 December with Gen McAuliffe on the left and Col Steve Chappius in the centre, wearing his Silver Star. /*US Army*

The last two days of 1944 saw two separate struggles. South-west of Bastogne two fresh American divisions, the 11th Armored and 87th Infantry, attacked to widen the corridor into Bastogne and crashed into a simultaneous German counter-attack, launched by Panzer Lehr and the 26th Volksgrenadiers. After some hard fighting and considerable losses on both sides, the German divisions pulled back to their start lines. At the same time the 1st SS Panzer and the 167th Volksgrenadier Divisions tried to cut the corridor into Bastogne by breaking through the American 35th and 26th

Infantry Divisions from the east, but were driven back with the loss of 55 tanks by a combination of ground fire and concentrated air attacks by the US XIX Tactical Air Command. On 30 December Gen Patton drove into Bastogne to congratulate the garrison and pinned the Distinguished Service Cross on Brig-Gen McAuliffe and Col Steve Chappuis.

At Supreme Headquarters in Paris Gen Eisenhower received on 30 December Field Marshal Montgomery's comments on Ike's directive for future operations, ending with yet another repetition of Monty's insistence on being given overall operational control over both his own 21st Army Group and Gen Bradley's 12th Army Group. This was too much for even the patient Eisenhower and he now decided that either he or Monty must go. A message to this effect was drafted for the Combined Chiefs of Staff, but before it could be sent, Monty's Chief of Staff at 21st Army Group, Maj Gen Francis de Guingand, arrived at SHAEF. De Guingand, already warned by reports from his liaison officer at 12th Army Group of American hostility to Monty and his ideas, had that same morning telephoned Ike's Chief of Staff, Bedell Smith and was made aware of the critical state of affairs.

Flying with his American pilot, Jack Race, through appalling weather to Orly airfield, de Guingand heard from Ike himself the seriousness of the situation and read Ike's draft signal to the Combined Chiefs of Staff. Freddie de Guingand assured Gen Eisenhower that Monty had no idea that he was causing so much upset and persuaded him to hold the signal for 24 hours. Next day de Guingand flew to Monty's tactical headquarters at Tongres in Belgium and shocked Monty into realising that he was in imminent danger of the sack. There was no question of replacing Eisenhower, as the British could now only field 17 or 18 divisions and the Americans were contributing far more men and armaments to the war effort. De Guingand then produced a signal, already drafted, for Monty to sign, promising full cooperation and asking Ike to destroy the earlier letter which had caused the storm. This was signed and sent off and the affair ended with an amicable exchange of letters all round.

Freddie de Guingand's day was not yet over, however. He drove back that night to 21st Army Group Main Headquarters in Brussels to brief a press conference of senior war correspondents, chaired by Alan Moorehead. De Guingand told them the whole story and stressed the need for the British press to drop their quite inaccurate line that an incompetent American command had been saved by Monty's intervention.

In spite of de Guingand's prompt and effective action, made possible by his personal friendship with Bedell Smith and his own expertise and experience as a staff officer, there was a further row to come. At a press conference on 7 January, a week later, Monty underlined his loyalty to Ike and paid a tribute to American soldiers, but his chirpy description of his own part in the battle led the British press once again to publicise the view, that Monty had saved the day. A furious Bradley issued his own press statement and the row only really ended, when Mr Churchill made a moving speech in the House of Commons on 17 January making clear that the Ardennes was 'an ever-famous American victory'.

Monty himself later agreed in his book 'Normandy to the Baltic', that 'a vital contribution to the slowing down of the enemy's advance was the dogged resistance of isolated American groups at main, nodal points, particularly St Vith and Bastogne' – but some years later in his Memoirs he wrote: 'The battle would never have

happened, if we had fought the campaign properly after Normandy or had tactical balance. We lost six weeks – with all that that entailed in political consequences at the end of the war' and so returned to his long quest for overall command of the Allied land forces in North-West Europe.

Final plans for the Allies' counter-attack were completed at the meeting in Hasselt on 28 December between Gen Eisenhower and Field Marshal Montgomery. Gen Patton's orders, given him at Verdun on 19 December to drive through Bastogne to Houffalize, were confirmed and the attack from the north would now be carried out by Gen Collins' VII Corps astride the Liège-Bastogne road, through Manhay and the Baraque de Fraiture crossroads to Houffalize and a meeting with Patton's Third Army.

British troops from Gen Horrocks' XXX Corps would relieve the American 2nd Armored and 84th Infantry Divisions west of the River Ourthe, to free these two divisions for the attack. Some Americans, embittered by the transfer to Monty's command of the US First Army and the subsequent wrangling over his press conference, complained that this fresh, British corps should take a more active part in the fighting, but Monty held to his plan and XXX Corps played a comparatively minor role in the new offensive. He was right to do this, as there were no more British divisions available and his 21st Army Group were still to face bitter fighting and heavy casualties in the New Year, clearing the west bank of the Rhine from Holland to the Ruhr. To have launched a British corps into an attack now further east in the Ardennes would also have meant maintaining it right across existing American lines of communication in difficult country and on an inadequate road net.

On 1 January 1945 the Americans saluted the New Year at one minute past midnight by firing all their artillery for 20 minutes in an intense bombardment of German positions throughout the Ardennes, causing heavy casualties. The Germans, too, celebrated New Year's Day by a comprehensive attack on 13 British and four American tactical airfields by more than a thousand German aircraft. Flying low and in wireless silence, they surprised the Allied defences and destroyed 150 aircraft, damaging 111 more and killing 46 men, six of them in air combat. But it was an expensive operation for the Luftwaffe. 260 German aircrew lost their lives and 280 planes were destroyed.

Among the British casualties was Monty's personal aircraft, a United States Army Air Corps Dakota, destroyed on the ground.

Below: The 75th Division move forward to relieve the 82nd Airborne. men of the 291st Infantry./*US Army*

Right: The Royal Welch Fusiliers moving towards Marche./*IWM*

Below: Field Marshal Montgomery, newly appointed Colonel Commandant of the Parachute Regiment with Maj-Gen Eric Bols, commanding the 6th Airborne Division, and behind them the three brigade commanders, Flavell, Hill and Poett and the battalion commanders. (Author in top left corner!) /*IWM*

Bottom: A patrol in the Ardennes wearing snow-suits, made out of village bed-linen. /*IWM*

Gen Eisenhower ordered its immediate replacement, underlining not only his own generosity of spirit, but the reluctance of the RAF to provide proper support for senior Army commanders in command and liaison flying.

Between Christmas and the New Year the British XXX Corps moved up to the neighbourhood of Marche and were joined there by the 6th Airborne Division from England, where they had been retraining and building up their strength after heavy casualties in Normandy. The Division left Salisbury Plain on Christmas Eve moving by sea and road transport and took over defensive positions west of Marche from the American 84th Infantry Division. The 9th Parachute Battalion held Humain and the wooded ridge overlooking the bare slopes down to the Marche-Rochefort railway, which marked the line of the German positions. Digging-in was made difficult by the presence of marble quarries along the ridge and in the night temperature of 28 degrees of frost, the men slept in their slit-trenches, piled on top of each other.

Battalion headquarters were more comfortably established in the village estaminet with a roaring fire, where their highly effective, supporting gunner battery commander, a High Court judge in later life, appropriated the bar itself as his office and spent most of the 24 hours on a camp-bed behind the bar, fully dressed on top but wearing pyjama trousers below – much to the surprise of visiting generals.

Above: A section of the 53rd Welsh Division.
/*IWM*

Left: More men of the 53rd Division moving up towards Marche./*IWM*

Below left: A Vickers machine gun section of B Company, 2nd Manchesters, in action near Marche./*IWM*

Above right: Some of the 290th Infantry, 75th Division in action at Beffe – with a cameraman handy!/*US Army*

Right: A German anti-tank gun in Malempré, with its crew dead beside it./*US Army*

Patrols each night in requisitioned sheets located the German positions, but by day nothing moved over the snow-covered fields. On the third morning a three-ton truck from another division drove straight through the battalion lines and before anyone could stop it, went motoring down the country road towards Hargimont and the enemy. At the level-crossing the many eyes glued to binoculars saw some Germans run out of a signalbox and drag the driver from the cab, but as the ground behind them was fully exposed to British fire they could only move out of their signalbox position at night. After some discussion on how to rescue the driver, the gunner called a 5.5in medium battery by radio and for three hours steadily ranged a single gun on to the signalbox. Finally he hit it with a big, black shell-burst to the cheers of the watching battalion. A flurry of Germans scattered up the far hill-side, followed by a shower of bullets, and a lone figure began to run up the slope towards the British positions. To more cheering a very breathless Royal Army Service Corps driver finally made it and fell into the nearest slit trench.

The British XXX Corps now prepared to advance on the right of the American VII Corps with the 53rd Welsh Division leading on the left and the 6th Airborne on the right. On 3 January the Allied attacks began in fog and mud, as a temporary thaw set in.

Above left: Churchill tanks, waiting to move forward in support of the 53rd Division./*IWM*

Left: 2nd Battalion The Monmouthshire Regiment on the march./*IWM*

Above: A group of the East Lancashires, before their attack on Grimbiemont./*IWM*

Right: The 7th Black Watch in Hotton./*IWM*

Below: . . . here astonishing the children. /*IWM*

Severe frost and heavy snowfalls in the days that followed, made movement easier for tanks, but helped to conceal the extensive German minefields. The weather also hindered Allied air support, German resistance was stubborn and Allied progress was slow. The Americans gained only two miles that first day, the 2nd Armored Division with the 335th Infantry taking Beffe and the 3rd Armored reaching Floret and Malempré. On the British left the 53rd Division advanced to clear the enemy from the country south of Marche as far as La Roche, supported by 11 regiments of artillery and one of tanks. They were resisted by the 116th Panzer Division, who counter-attacked several times and it took a full scale battalion attack by the 1st Battalion the East Lancashire Regiment to capture Grimbiemont on 7 January, only four miles from Marche. On 8 January the 51st Highland Division took over the lead from the 53rd and as the Germans began to withdraw to the east, the advance quickened. On 11 January the Scotsmen were in La Roche and a few days later a British patrol from XXX Corps made contact with Americans, moving north from the Third Army just south of La Roche.

On the right of XXX Corps the British 6th Airborne Division's

Left: A British and an American patrol meet south of Laroche./*IWM*

Below: British manned Sherman tanks, probably the 23rd Hussars, near Rochefort. /*IWM*

Right: Company B, 325th Glider Infantry, move forward once more./*US Army*

Below right: Men of the 504th Parachute Infantry advancing./*US Army*

5th Parachute Brigade had had a hard fight in Bures on 3 January, bitterly defended by the Panzer Lehr Division. The 13th Parachute Battalion and the 23rd Hussars attacked at 1.30pm, but A Company was caught by German artillery and mortar fire on their start-line. Maj Watson led them on into the village, but B Company in moving round the village to the high ground beyond it, were met by intense fire from tanks, assault guns and infantry. All three platoon commanders and the company sergeant-major were killed, and soon there were only 21 men left on their feet. A German counter-attack was held up by Lt Lagergern, hurling grenades, until he was killed, but the village was only cleared by Maj Reeves Clarke's C Company at about 5pm.

Next day, 4 January, the Panzer Lehr counter-attacked again and again, but were beaten back each time by artillery, tank and infantry fire and finally the arrival of Maj Granville's glider company from the 52nd Light Infantry made the village secure. It had been a costly fight, for the 13th Battalion had lost seven officers and 182 soldiers killed and wounded and 16 of the 23rd Hussars' tanks had been knocked out. During the first day's fighting, when half the village was still in German hands, Scott, the battalion's medical sergeant, took a stretcher jeep forward into Bures to pick up casualties. As he was doing this a big Jagdtiger – an 88mm assault gun – clanked round the corner and pulled up beside him. The German commander opened his hatch, looked at Scott and said: 'Take the wounded away this time, but don't come back. It's not safe.' Sergeant Scott, who had won that rare decoration, the Distinguished Conduct Medal, was killed in the last few weeks of the war at Wunsdorf in Germany.

Left: Some of the murdered men of Bandes soon after discovery./*IWM*

Below left: Identification begins./*US Army*

Right: The coffins are laid out in line, draped with the Belgian flag, by men of the 9th Parachute Battalion./*IWM*

Below: The funeral procession to the village church./*IWM*

Below right: The funeral mass./*IWM*

In front of the 3rd Parachute Brigade the Germans withdrew without fighting and the only incident was the entry into the village of Bandes of the 9th Parachute Battalion an hour or so after the Germans had left. The village gave the battalion a subdued welcome and were obviously short of food. Only women, children and old men were visible and they said that all the young and middle-aged men had been taken away after church on Christmas Day for forced labour, as a reprisal for guerilla activity in the region. The Germans had also burned down the lower half of the village, through which ran the main road,

The battalion shook out into a defensive position and patrols went off to reconnoitre the neighbouring woods. One of them came back almost at once with the shocking news of finding a pile of bodies in the burned out part of the village on the main road,

all shot through the back of the head. These were the men of the village and there now fell to the battalion the sad task of telling the villagers of their loss and of getting them to identify the bodies. The battalion snipers went out into the woods to shoot deer for the village foodstocks; the pioneers set to work to make coffins; the padre and all the men did what they could to comfort the people; and a mass burial service was held – and all through this time of personal and collective grief, every house in the village made the soldiers welcome with a coffee or a cognac or simply a chair to sit down in.

By 16 January the whole of the British XXX Corps were moving back northwards to rejoin 21st Army Group and to prepare for the next task of clearing the west bank of the Rhine from Holland to the Ruhr.

In the American sector 4 January saw the 82nd Airborne Division advancing towards Salmchateau and taking 500 prisoners. By the 7th the 84th Infantry Division were in Marcouray and the 2nd Armored had recaptured the battlefields of Dochamps and Baraque de Fraiture. By now even Hitler had begun to realise the hard facts of Allied superiority and on 9 January he authorised the withdrawal of the Fifth Panzer Army to positions east of the Liege – Bastogne road. The Sixth SS Panzer Army were ordered into reserve north of St Vith, but such was the chaos on the roads and tracks caused by the weather and Allied air strikes, that it took them four more days to get there. German soldiers still fought stubbornly and with their usual skill, but morale was beginning to crack. In spite of the fact that the SS divisions were going back into reserve for transfer to the dreaded Eastern front, their withdrawal was resented by Army units, who regarded it as favouritism for the SS. Rations were now reduced, home leave was cut, reprisals against the families of deserters were threatened, mail hardly ever appeared and rumours multiplied of the widespread damage and casualties at home from the bombing of German cities – and in every German soldier's mind was the mounting fear of Russian invasion.

On 9 January the American Third Army launched their main offensive with four infantry divisions – the 26th, 35th, 87th and 90th – two armoured divisions – the 4th and 6th – and the 101st

and 17th Airborne Divisions. They made slow progress and the 90th Division suffered heavy casualties. The 101st Airborne attacked northwards towards Noville, but it took them six days to cover those five miles. Julian Ewell, whose 501st Parachute Infantry had stopped Panzer Lehr at Neffe on 19 December, was an early casualty in this new attack, wounded in the foot and leg.

The German divisions, now weak in men and weapons, fought desperately to hold the Allied advances form north and south. In the north the 116th Panzers and the 12th, 560th and 32nd Volksgrenadiers struggled to slow the drive towards Houffalize of the American VII Corps and inflicted 1,600 casualties on the 83rd Division. In the south the Panzer Lehr, 3rd and 15th Panzer Grenadier, 5th Parachute and 167th Volksgrenadiers fought against Patton's Third Army, but slowly and inexorably they were driven back.

On 12 January the Soviet winter offensive began on a massive scale and two days later Hitler ordered the Sixth SS Panzer Army to move east, but to Gen Guderian's disgust, into Hungary to protect the oilfields, rather than to Prussia's eastern border. On 15 January the 84th Infantry Division took Houffalize and the American First and Third Armies joined hands once more. Two days later, on 17 January, the US First Army reverted to 12th Army Group under Gen Bradley's command and by 27 January the American lines were back to where they had been, when the German offensive had begun on 16 December. The Battle of the Bulge was over.

It was certainly an American victory. Three German armies had attacked five United States divisions on a front of 50 miles. Yet within four days half a million Allied soldiers were moving towards the Ardennes. The losses on both sides were heavy. Between the opening bombardment of 16 December and the end of January, 8,497 United States soldiers and airmen fell in battle, 46,170 more were wounded and 20,905 were reported as missing, some of whom were dead, but most of whom were prisoners of war. But already by 2 January 31,000 American reinforcements had reached the battle front. Here lay the crucial difference. German casualty figures are

Left: A King Tiger is used as a signal pole by men of the 82nd Airborne Division./*US Army*

Below left: A German tank still burning after a hit from a 7th Armored Division tank in the advance to re-capture St Vith. The photographer, Technician Hugh McHugh, was killed shortly after taking this photograph./*US Army*

Below: Company C, 23rd Armored Infantry reach Hunnange in the drive for St Vith./*US Army*

Above left: Another view of the advance – tanks moving through Didenberg./*US Army*

Left: Half-tracks of the 6th Armored Division prepare to advance near Bastogne./*US Army*

Above: The 48th Armored Infantry, back once more in St Vith with the rest of the 7th Armored Division./*US Army*

difficult to discover, but they certainly lost 50,000 men in the Ardennes as prisoners of war and their dead have been estimated at nearly 13,000. Another estimate from German sources is an overall loss of 92,000 men, killed, wounded and missing – but whatever the actual figures, the German losses were severe and could not now be replaced. Nor could the hundreds of tanks and assault guns lying wrecked in the snow of the Ardennes.

Since the end of World War II the Russians have claimed that it was their winter offensives in the east, beginning on 12 January 1945, which saved the Allied armies in the west from defeat. They have pointed to Sir Winston Churchill's telegram to Stalin of 6 January, in which he asked for a prompt beginning to the Russian offensive, as contributory evidence of this.

Yet the reverse is probably true. There were more German tanks and guns in the Ardennes during December and early January, than in the whole of the Eastern Front. Certainly the complete collapse of German resistance once the Allies had crossed the Rhine was largely due to the huge German losses in men and material in the Ardennes and Reichswald battles.

The German High Command achieved complete surprise on 16 December but however good the leadership of Model and Manteuffel and their panzer commanders they never came near to achieving either Hitler's distant targets of Brussels and Antwerp or their own more limited aims of splitting the American and British Armies. The Allies' speed of reaction was too fast, the power of the American and British Air Forces was too great, once the weather had cleared on 23 December and the American soldier had fought too well at the northern shoulder, in the cauldron of St Vith, during the siege of Bastogne and in all those detachments of infantry, engineers, tanks and guns, who had held on to their own isolated bridge or crossroads.

Above: Men of the 3rd Armored Division
race into a village under fire./*US Army*

Above Right: A patrol from the 17th Airborne
Division, after a 20 mile march, meets men of
the VII Corps, 24th Cavalry, near LaRoche
– one of the first link-ups between the US
First and Third Armies – on 14 January.
/*US Army*

Right: Another link-up – here a patrol from
the 84th Infantry Division in the First Army,
meets another from the 11th Armored Division
in the Third Army at the Ourthe river.
/*US Army*

Bibliography

Hugh M. Coie; *The United States Army in World War II: The Ardennes – Battle of the Bulge*; Office of the Chief of Military History, 1965

John S. D. Eisenhower; *The Bitter Woods*; G. P. Putnam's Sons, New York, 1969

Brig-Gen S. L. A. Marshall; *The First Eight Days*; Infantry Journal Press, 1946

Charles Whiting; *Massacre at Malmedy*; Leo Cooper, 1971

Maj L. F. Ellis and Lt-Col A. E. Warhurst; *History of the Second World War:-Victory in the West Vol II*; HMSO 1968

Robert E. Merriam; *Battle of the Bulge*; Panther Books

John Toland; *Battle – The Story of the Bulge*; Frederick Muller, London

Sir Winston Churchill; *The Second World War, Vol VI*; Cassell, 1954

Chester Wilmot; *The Struggle for Europe*; Collins, 1952

Maj-Gen Sir Francis de Guingand; *Operation Victory*; Hodder and Stoughton, 1947

Field Marshal Viscount Montgomery of Alamein; *Normandy to the Baltic*; BAOR, 1946

Field Marshal Viscount Montgomery of Alamein; *Memoirs*; Collins, 1958

Hitler's Generals and Their Battles; Salamander Books

James Jones; *Graphic Art of World War II*; Leo Cooper

Ronald Heiferman; *World War II*; Octopus Books

R. J. T. Hills; *Phantom was There*; Edward Arnold and Co, 1951

Winston G. Ramsey; *After the Battle No 4*; Battle of Britain Prints Limited

Joss Heintz; *In the Perimeter of Bastogne*; Omnia, Ostend, 1965

Index